Esports Insights

Esports Insights outlines the fundamental characteristics, features, and structures of the rapidly growing esports industry and acts as the perfect primer for readers without any prior knowledge of esports.

Featuring international case studies in every chapter, this book showcases the contemporary nature of esports through illustrative, industry examples. By offering a concise and easy to understand introduction, it discusses the key components, stakeholders, and features of this commercially driven sector, which by its very nature is dynamic and highly complex. Exploring current regulatory and governance structures within esports, this text unpacks the industry's essential features by outlining the various genres, formats, and stakeholders who are instrumental to the functioning of the esports industry. Adopting a critical but balanced analysis, the book discusses the social benefits of esports, outlining its potential as a tool for social inclusion and sport development, whilst acknowledging the potential impacts and risks of esports participation and spectatorship, related to health and wellbeing. Finally, *Esports Insights* considers future developments and changes within esports, as the sector evolves and continues to professionalise.

This book will be of interest to any student, researcher, or practitioner with an interest in sport business, sport and society, event studies, esports or video gaming, or the wider media industry.

Emily Hayday is Lecturer at Loughborough University London, UK and is based within the Institute for Sport Business.

Emily Collison-Randall is Senior Lecturer at Loughborough University London, UK and is based within the Institute for Sport Business.

Sarah Kelly OAM is Associate Professor at the University of Queensland, Australia, a Visiting fellow at Loughborough University London, UK and a non-executive director in the sport and tourism sectors.

Sport Business Insights
Series Editors
Aaron C.T. Smith, *Loughborough University, UK*
Constantino Stavros, *RMIT University, Australia*

Sport Business Insights is a series that aims to cut through the clutter, providing concise and relevant introductions to an array of contemporary topics related to the business of sport. Readers – including passionate practitioners, curious consumers and sport students alike – will discover direct and succinct volumes, carefully curated to present a useful blend of practice and theory. In a highly readable format, and prepared by leading experts, this series shines a spotlight on subjects of currency in sport business, offering a systematic guide to critical concepts and their practical application.

Available in this series:

Sport Branding Insights
Constantino Stavros and Aaron C.T. Smith

Sport Sponsorship Insights
Norm O'Reilly, Gashaw Abeza and Mark Harrison

Esports Insights
Emily Hayday, Holly Collison-Randall, and Sarah Kelly

For more information about this series, please visit: *www.routledge.com*

Esports Insights

Emily Hayday, Holly Collison-Randall, and Sarah Kelly

Routledge
Taylor & Francis Group

LONDON AND NEW YORK

First published 2022
by Routledge
4 Park Square, Milton Park, Abingdon, Oxon OX14 4RN

and by Routledge
605 Third Avenue, New York, NY 10158

Routledge is an imprint of the Taylor & Francis Group, an informa business

British Library Cataloguing-in-Publication Data
A catalogue record for this book is available from the British Library

Library of Congress Cataloging-in-Publication Data
Names: Hayday, Emily, author. | Collison-Randall, Holly, author. |
    Kelly, Sarah (Sarah Jane), author.
Title: Esports insights / Emily Hayday, Holly Collison-Randall,
    Sarah Kelly.
Description: Abingdon, Oxon ; New York, NY : Routledge, 2022. |
    Series: Sport business insights | Includes bibliographical references
    and index.
Identifiers: LCCN 2021057794 | ISBN 9781032044279 (hardback) |
    ISBN 9781032100890 (paperback) | ISBN 9781003213598 (ebook)
Subjects: LCSH: eSports (Contests) | eSports (Contests)—
    Economic aspects.
Classification: LCC GV1469.34.E86 H39 2022 | DDC
    794.8—dc23/eng/20211222
LC record available at https://lccn.loc.gov/2021057794

ISBN: 978-1-032-04427-9 (hbk)
ISBN: 978-1-032-10089-0 (pbk)
ISBN: 978-1-003-21359-8 (ebk)

DOI: 10.4324/9781003213598

Typeset in Times New Roman
by Apex CoVantage, LLC

Contents

Preface

As sports enthusiasts, consumers, and scholars we often look to numbers and statistics to inform us of trends and areas of growth or decline. The numbers and statistics associated with esports leave little space for doubt of its place in the sport sector and mainstream popular cultures. In 2020, 435.9 million people around the world watched esports events, increasing that was 10% from 397 million in 2019 (Debusmann Jr, 2021). At the same time, esports worldwide revenues hit $947 million in 2020, driven by sponsorship from global brands. These figures are only an indicator of exponential growth, estimated to reach viewing figures of 474 million by 2021, which is coupled with global esports revenues increasing to $1,084 million in 2021, with a year-on-year growth of plus 14.5% (Newzoo, 2021). The numbers provide a snapshot of the rate in which esports has engaged increasingly diverse audiences, connected more broadly to mainstream sports and the entertainment industry, and esports intensifying relationships with commercial partners. Such data means that it is critical to recognise that esports is no longer an emerging enterprise, but rather a cornerstone of the entertainment and wider sport industry. But what does this mean for esports athletes, user groups, fans, publishers, corporate partners, and industries that recognise the value of its diverse platforms?

Such questions are timely. Esports are no longer bound by isolated playing formats and virtual environments but are now interconnected and transnationally connected in multiple ways. This links to the notion of esports acting as a digital mediator, with the evolving esports landscape characterised by a convergence of industries and multiple stakeholders in digital environments. Esports are at the forefront of this evolution and are breaking the barriers between sport, technology, fashion, business, and entertainment. Digital mediation via esports offers new opportunities and challenges for many stakeholders and organisations who are looking to engage, assimilate, leverage, and build connections with audiences who occupy these spaces. Secondly, the focus on esports as a tool and driver for social change is important. This has three unique elements: firstly, as a digital mediator, esports prominent position heightens accountability and will need a more public social conscious, secondly, esports are increasingly drawn into global social development agendas like the United Nations Sustainable Development Goals, and thirdly, to maintain a USP within the wider sport business landscape. Although *Esports Insights* take a critical stance, we believe esports are wide ranging, and underutilised, the value and opportunities for esports to be a vehicle for positive outcomes is yet to be fully realised. Throughout this book we look to highlight and drive insights that make connections for esports ability to contribute to development challenges, agendas, and social goals.

Esports Insights offers succinct and valuable insights into the complex and nascent esports industry, by discussing the evolving and powerful realities of the contemporary esports domain. Considering the recent global pandemic, esports has transformed the trajectory of the sport and entertainment industry by providing virtual and online spaces for individuals and fans to engage. Esports presents significant opportunities post-COVID-19 to both the traditional sports industry and beyond, across cultural, economic, and social domains. Therefore, *Esports Insights* explains the fundamental characteristics, features, and structures of the esports industry. There is still limited consensus and awareness of what esports embodies, due to its unique characteristics, multiple formats, and fragmented nature, resulting in the need for this text, as many (students, practitioners, and academics) look to develop a richer understanding of what esports is and the specific challenges and opportunities that this complex and relatively new domain provides. The authors of this book draw upon their expertise and experience in the fields of governance, sociology, esports research, and sport business to provide insights into the esports landscape at a time when both opportunities for collaboration and driving social change, and challenges to governance and welfare are dominating esports discourse.

For example, a consequence of esports' rise is the uptake of its various platforms by elite sport organisations, entertainment companies, music events, global policymakers, the education section, civil society organisations, and fashion brands. Esports are no longer a sporting platform vying for acceptance within mainstream sporting contexts but a viable and much desired fan engagement strategy, educational tool, information sharing instrument, and partner of performance sport clubs. Esports is a complex industry that is currently being pushed and pulled in different directions, arguably the pull towards intersecting commercial, social and education spaces is pushing esports away from its desires for legitimacy within the mainstream sporting landscape. But does esports inherently have a problem? Is its fractured nature and lack of universal consensus fuelling governance issues and welfare concerns? At the same time, does the freedom and flexibility of esports enhance its ability to drive social change? Is esports itself the pioneer of inclusive sporting practice? Therefore, this seems like an opportune time to reflect, take stock, and consider the future of the esports industry. We use these guiding questions to frame the main sections of this book and use empirical data, case studies, and research to highlight the complexities and consider future directions for the esports industry.

Esports' lucrative appeal is drawing attention from many stakeholders looking to understand how they could be part of the esports landscape. Therefore, the focus of this book will be of value not only to sport management students, but also to practitioners and organisations who are exploring the potential and navigating the 'unknowns' of the esports industry. *Esports Insights* is intended to provide readers who have limited or no previous knowledge, education, or experience within the area with a practical and useful introduction to esports.

The content seeks to support enthusiasts, scholars, and practitioners who have no previous experience of esports, by introducing foundational knowledge and key aspects of the industry, alongside highlighting its potential within the broader sports industry and beyond. This ensures insights are self-contained in nature and is suitable for practitioners and post-secondary and undergraduate level students. The authors recognise that in its infant state, readers will have a varied experience of esports nuances and therefore the text has been written with this in mind ensuring accessibility. The authors have committed to going beyond academic discourse and have pursued highly practical insights and points of reference, only drawing and referring to fundamental principles, practical examples, and unique components of the esports space. Readers' knowledge and understanding of the esports sector will increase incrementally throughout this text, providing a comprehensive understanding for any individual who is new to the esports space.

Organisation and structure

Constructed through five main sections, each is framed around a pertinent theme and at the start three key questions are positioned to the reader. These act as the guiding priorities for each chapter and will be answered through the forthcoming content within each section. Throughout, the authors draw upon internationally relevant case studies to add novel insights and ensure relevant understanding by showcasing practical, industry-based examples.

Chapter 1. *Esports fundamentals* focuses on the key concepts, characteristics, and features of esports, which provides the reader with the foundational understanding of the sector. Esports has proliferated the entertainment and sports sectors, becoming a cornerstone of the digital environment, yet this complex industry is multifaceted, and this chapter will outline the multiple genres and formats that esports can take. Focus will be placed on outlining the key stakeholders who contribute to and sustain the burgeoning esports industry. Chapter 1 also explores the digital space in which esports resides, which has led to new forms of consumption, where the boundaries between content consumption and creation are blurred. The evolving nature of sport, media, and entertainment, means that esports is positioned at an intersect of these domains and this chapter concludes by outlining how esports could be conceptualised as a 'digital mediator'.

Chapter 2. *Esports governance and regulation* introduces fundamental insights into the current business models and governance practices that are undertaken within esports. Critically, the distinct context of esports may mean that traditional sports governance approaches may not be applicable or aligned with the needs of the sector. Evidence suggests impact and reach of esports influences and risk are vast and there is a pressing need for ethical regulation and trusted enforcement. Governance structures and organisations have been created, and although they provide some oversight and mitigation of these risks, they are challenged by lack of jurisdiction across leagues and tournaments, conflicts of interest, and limited implementation. Chapter 2 outlines key areas for policy and governance intervention, including e-doping and doping, match fixing, athlete rights, microtransactions in game, and labour issues. Models of governance and examples are discussed, from self-regulation to independent governance approaches, and policy intervention. The complex and uniquely digital environment of esports is emphasised, along with the need to balance commercial and social objectives.

Chapter 3. *Esports as a mechanism for social change* reveals the opportunities and potential that esports provides not only for those involved in the industry, but for stakeholders within the sport industry and beyond. Social change in the context of esports has nuanced dimensions compared to traditional sporting activities and outcomes. Esports provides opportunities for cross-cultural communication and opportunities for social change interventions that span global contexts and populations. The broad concept of social change is multi-faceted and goes beyond the assumption that social interaction results in social change outcomes. In simple terms, sport (esports and mainstream) can bring people together but how can this lead to behaviour change, heightened awareness of civic responsibility, education and skill development, and community building? Chapter 3 highlights that social interaction is simply the initial step in creating and strengthening social change impacts and that esports can add to traditional social change offerings via innovative and virtually driven theories of change.

Chapter 4. *Esports health and wellbeing* outlines the important considerations and characteristics of esports engagement, by outlining positive and negative health and wellbeing impacts associated with online gaming spaces. Chapter 4 considers the addictive nature and various framings of esports as a 'mental disorder', before illustrating how the COVID-19 pandemic accelerated esports growth, through the need for digital engagement through esports global virtual communities. Mental health and physical activity and their importance are discussed, as components of positive esports participation, and examples of how esports stakeholders are supporting this agenda are provided. Future growth areas within esports such as gambling and in game microtransactions are explored, these activities can act as a trigger for wellbeing concerns, especially through the possible impact on vulnerable youth participants. This suggests that esports participants and fans are vulnerable and at risk from over, and unregulated, exposure to gambling that can lead to significant long-term welfare concerns.

Finally, Chapter 5. *Esports evolution* reflects on key changes and trends that will inform the future of esports. The exponential growth trajectory of esports is predicted to continue, particularly driven by mainstream media accessibility, penetration into new markets through mobile and increasing sponsorship and proprietary revenues. The growing diversification strategy by traditional sport into esports is also showcased as a brand extension strategy. Chapter 5 examines the rise of esports influencers, a trend set to continue with the changing consumption behaviours of next generation audiences, adoption of ad blocking software and authenticity of esports celebrities. Technological advancements and innovation in esports are outlined, which will further broaden engagement and market growth of esports, along with economic impacts. Conclusions place emphasis upon the need for reliable governance of esports, to ensure positive growth of the sector, the protection of vulnerable participants and to enable the esports sector to enact its social potential.

Consequently, this book aims to demystify the esports space by providing a concise and comprehensive overview of the esports domain. Primarily, focus will be placed on key concepts, characteristics, and definitions as the foundational framing of the evolving esports landscape and its cultural relevance and position within today's digitalised world. Opportunities and considerations related to governance, health, and social domains will be exposed to provide the reader with a holistic understanding of the value and complexity of the bourgeoning esports industry. This book offers an accessible, highly practical text for any reader looking to enhance their familiarity, knowledge, and expertise around the area of esports.

References

Debusmann Jr, B. (2021, March 15). Interest in e-sports will only grow and grow. *BBC News.* www.bbc.co.uk/news/business-56334015

Newzoo. (2021, March 9). Newzoo's global esports & live streaming market report 2021. *Newzoo.* https://newzoo.com/insights/trend-reports/newzoos-global-esports-live-streaming-market-report-2021-free-version

Acknowledgements

Firstly, to our incredible contributors who made this book possible. Without your insights, case studies, and expertise this text would not have been possible. We would also like to share our gratitude with the series editors Professor Aaron Smith and Associate Professor Con Stavros for the opportunity to contribute *Esports Insights* to this series.

Finally, I would like to thank my co-authors Holly and Sarah, it has been a pleasure working with you both and I look forward to our future research ventures.

1   Esports fundamentals

Key Questions

1. *What are the key characteristics, engagement modes, and definition of esports?*
2. *Who are the key stakeholders involved in the esports industry?*
3. *What role does esports have within a digital environment?*

Introduction

This chapter provides insight into the world of esports, by outlining the key features, components, and attributes of the industry. COVID-19 accelerated engagement with esports as alternative forms of entertainment were not possible and the virtual environment in which esports is situated offers a unique position unbounded by location or social restrictions. Esports has transformed the trajectory of the sport, media, and entertainment industries by providing virtual and online spaces for individuals and fans to engage, connect, consume, and create. The sector has expanded from its online gaming foundations to a cultural, commercial, and globally positioned industry, offering significant economic and social impact, which is attracting lucrative investment. It is not just a recreational and high-performance platform, but a business which resonates with younger generations, and with this, global brands are keen to reach the next generation consumers through esports.

Media and streaming platforms such as Tik Tok, Instagram, YouTube, and Twitch have resulted in a new digital environment, where individuals are connecting, creating, and consuming content online. The ability for fans and consumers to create content that can be enjoyed and shared has resulted in a shift in value creation. Historically, individuals were delivered information and content through traditional media consumption models (TV and linear broadcasting), whereas digital and social media platforms allow

DOI: 10.4324/9781003213598-1

interactivity and reciprocal engagement, meaning users become part of content creation process, rather than passive consumers. Typically, esports are accessed via consoles, mobile or personal computers, and can be played or streamed anywhere, facilitated by any devices connected to the internet. In recent years mobile esports popularity has increased, which opens up esports to new audiences and modes of engagement, due to the heightened flexibility that mobile devices allow, whilst also reducing entry barriers as specialist equipment (PC or console) is not required.

What is esports?

Electronic sports or esports originated in Stanford University's Artificial Intelligence Laboratory in 1972, with a group of students gathering to play Spacewar, one of the world's first video games. Esports started as an underground culture with gamers organising Local Area Network (LAN) parties and building their own communities from the ground up. Esports has now grown into a billion-dollar industry, attracting a global audience of over 500 million (as both participants and spectators), establishing it within digital youth culture.

Esports in its broadest sense can be defined as competitive online video gaming and although not a new concept, the interest, popularity, and acknowledgment of the esports sector has grown significantly in the 21st century. Esports is used as an umbrella term to describe a complex and evolving industry, which although positioned in a virtual environment, shares many characteristics with the traditional sports industry (Scholz, 2020). The esports industry has developed clear league and competition structures and franchises, organisational and business management practices, mainstream sponsorship and media support, and talent development pathways, however due to the composition and ownership structures there are specific governance and regulatory challenges, which are unique to this digitised industry (Peng et al., 2020).

Esports is a product of digital disruption, and the live streaming platform Twitch has been instrumental in the global development and reach of esports, by providing an online platform for gamers to discuss their views and opinions, around a shared interest. Twitch is the most popular streaming media platform, reaching 90% of total esports audiences, with many celebrity gamers streaming and communicating from multiple platforms including YouTube and social media, alongside Twitch. Streamers on Twitch live stream their gameplay, commentaries, and other activities by sharing their screen with subscribers and fans who watch them live, comment, and interact directly through the stream chat functionality. Online gaming and live streaming platforms such as Twitch and YouTube Gaming have become the go to environment for gamers, as they provide an interactive space for entertainment, social opportunities, and foster the creation of online communities.

The professional esports scene is unique in this respect, as the physical proximity between fans and the athletes during a competition or tournament is non-existent. Although in traditional sport, athletes have amassed millions of followers on different social channels and often share personal content from their lives outside of sport, when esports athletes are competing, apart from the crowd at the stadium, they do not have direct contact with fans for that period of competition. Yet, at esports events and competitions, afforded by the virtual environment and communication mechanisms, users can engage directly in real-time through the chat function with esports athletes and each other. Esports spaces allow instant connections and powerful interactions between different users, fans, and athletes that is not mirrored in other industries.

Esports origins as a cultural phenomenon started in South Korea but has become integrated into popular culture globally, especially amongst youth populations. With worldwide audiences in 2021 of 474.0 million, professional gamers are now seen as celebrities, competitions are being broadcast on national television networks, and industry revenues are expected to reach $1.8 billion in 2022, following a year-on-year growth trajectory of 15%. Esports has become a bourgeoning industry, experiencing an influx of brand investment and the emergence of esports services and creative industries associated with it. Even as early as 2006, Wagner (p. 1) described esports as a "fundamental element in today's digital youth culture" and the acceleration and interest in the sector illustrates the value and relevance of esports. Asia-Pacific, North America, and Europe are the top three global esports markets, with China specifically being the largest market for live streaming games, accumulating an audience of 193 million in 2021 (Newzoo, 2021). With a range of genres, game titles, and varying modes of engagement, what is esports?

Esports genres and formats

Esports, in its purest form, is an online activity where individuals compete against each other, depending on the game title there are multiple playing formats available, for example: 1v1, 2v2, 3v3, 4v4 and so forth. Esports is played at all levels, from amateur to professional and a common adage associated with esports is the principle of being "easy to learn, hard to master" (Scholz, 2020). Whether playing, spectating, or streaming esports has become an integral part of the daily lifestyle for millions across the globe. At the amateur level, there are relatively low barriers to entry, as esports can be played by anyone, regardless of gender, age, and physical ability. Although, as will be explored Chapter 4, entrenched norms and practices (often masculine and toxic) have shaped the cultures and customs currently seen within esports spaces, creating entry barriers for some individuals looking to engage with online competitive gaming.

Esports is a broad term that is often used to describe the sector; however, this is made up of multiple gaming titles, which can be characterised into esports genres. Funk et al. (2018) outline the most common which include: first-person shooter games (i.e., Global Offensive and Counterstrike), fighting games (i.e., StreetFighter, Smash Bros), multiplayer online battle arenas (i.e., League of Legends, DOTA 2), real-time strategy games (i.e., StarCraft), and sport-based video games (i.e., FIFA, Rocket League). The multiplicity and diversity of the esports landscape increases the popularity and engagement of different audiences. The dynamic and innovative nature of the industry alongside the appetite for new, immersive titles has resulted in a continuously evolving environment, with new games regularly being launched, to varying degrees of popularity. For example, Valorant is a free to play, first-person shooter game, that was developed by Riot Games and officially released in June 2020. A year on in 2021, Riot has confirmed an average of 14 million players globally are logging in each month to compete. A further example of the fluid and rapidly changing popularity and dominance of certain esports titles can be seen through the Epic Games title, Fortnite: Battle Royale, released in 2017, and free to download across numerous platforms. Fortnite was an overnight success and became the top selling app in numerous countries, attracting millions of gamers globally and achieving revenues of $1.5 million during its first week (Thompson, 2020).

To illustrate the popularity and scale of certain esports titles, The International is the annual esports world championship tournament for Dota 2. In 2019, this was hosted at the Mercedes-Benz Arena in Shanghai, China (last in-person tournament hosted as subsequent championships were postponed due to COVID-19) and this tournament achieved peak viewership of 1.97 million views and culminated in a prize pool of over US $34.3 million. Another global esports tournament, The Intel Extreme Masters in Katowice, Poland in 2019 attracted a live audience of over 174,000 fans across the tournaments, eclipsing live audiences seen in traditional sport (Cranmer et al., 2021).

Esports commercialisation

The community-driven origins of the esports industry have grown into a flourishing industry, which in 2021 generated $833.6 million in revenue (Newzoo, 2021). Commercialisation through in-game purchases, tickets, and merchandise sales contributed, yet media rights, advertising, and sponsorship accounted for over 75% of the total revenues in 2021 (Newzoo, 2021). Unlike traditional sport, esports have been built upon a purely commercial model, emanating from exclusive intellectual property ownership by game publishers. Revenue generation has grown beyond purchasing the game itself, with many free to play options, underpinned by subscription models, which are used to monetise certain formats and titles. Gaming structure has permitted creative revenue streams to be leveraged, through in-game microtransactions to elicit real world and virtual in game currency. Some of these currencies and chance-based rewards include virtual items such as, skins, loot boxes, personalisation of avatars, which are purchased in-game and do not offer any performance advantages. These highly popular virtual items instead offer cosmetic improvements in exchange for money and are specific to each esports title, for example, in Fortnite, 'V-Bucks' is the virtual currency used. Microtransactions form a key pillar of game publishers' commercialisation model and results in significant revenue generation. This form of gambling (purchasing virtual items) is proving extremely popular with young players, and controversial with regulators due to their gambling-like qualities and addictive potential (King & Delfabbro, 2019).

Appetite and interest in commercial investment within esports is continuing to grow as brands identify the valuable opportunities that esports offers for consumer engagement. Yet, for many brands esports is a new domain they are not familiar with, resulting in many grappling with the best way to engage and resonate with esports fans in authentic and meaningful ways. Trends, cultures, and value systems within the esports sector are unique to every game (i.e., League of Legends, Call of Duty, FIFA), with each title having its own community and specific identity. Therefore, for brands looking to enter this space it can be a complex and new environment to navigate. Agencies have in many ways stepped in to enhance understanding and knowledge around esports for many brands, who are looking to enter the esports space. The next case study outlines some of the work undertaken by DLC Studios, who works as a creative agency within the esports and gaming sphere.

Case Study: DLC Studios

Written by Daniel Chung – Director of Operations

DLC Studios is a creative agency focused on esports and gaming. We regularly work with brands such as Red Bull, ESL, and Ubisoft. Team members at DLC Studios all play, watch, and engage in the esports industry and working in the space allows us to be a part of and contribute to the very industry that we are passionate about. We want brands to have positive experiences within the esports industry and being engaged with esports ourselves means that we understand the communities and the cultures that have developed. This allows us to guide brands and help them create their own authentic content.

DLC Studios have undertaken a variety of work including video and photo work, graphics, and brand development. Case examples of our work show how our journey in esports has influenced and enabled us to create impactful work for our clients:

MNM Gaming – Brand development, world building, character design, merchandise design, packaging design, animation, video editing, and graphics design.

MNM Gaming is an esports club with a long history of competing in esports in the UK. DLC works with MNM Gaming to develop the brand that fully reflects its values. Through world building, character design, and content creation we have been able to help authentically represent what MNM stands for.

Red Bull Home Ground (Valorant) – Creative direction, logo design, and graphics design

Red Bull Home Ground (Valorant) is a tournament where teams select a map which becomes their "Home Ground". Beating a team on both your own and their home ground meant you won the game series and failing to do so meant you lost and are knocked out of the tournament. Visualising this tournament into a logo meant that we had to understand Valorant itself as a game. Playing Valorant prior to working on the logo allowed us to have a deeper appreciation for the game and allowed us to approach the concept with the right mindset. We visually based the logo on two maps, Bind and Icebox, and brought a hose of visual elements from the game to build the Red Bull Home Ground logo.

Work From Home (WFH) League - Creative direction, world concepting and design, brand development, logo design, graphics design, and animation.

WFH League started in 2020 with the intention of giving companies a platform to participate and engage in the esports space by competing in a tournament with others in a similar position. This meant the experiences of potential participators could range from very little to a lot and connecting to both everyone competing could prove challenging. Our approach was to build a world using visual imagery from retro gaming that anybody would have experience of which opened up the brand to connect with all participators.

Reflecting on the commercialisation of the esports industry and why brands are looking to enter the space, DLC Studios director Daniel Chung notes that:

Brand entry into esports has come about due to two trends, changing consumption behaviour and the effectiveness of established digital and non-digital advertising channels due to technological development. Traditionally sport has been an avenue for many brands to continuously engage with their consumer market to build and maintain brand affinity. However, over the recent years the average age of viewers of traditional sport has been increasing year on year. This shift is in part due to the rise of esports as an alternative entertainment to traditional sports, where the games are faster paced and more accessible in comparison. Accessibility of content has increased with the evolution of technology, which has evolved alongside consumption habits. People now have a wide range of entertainment at their fingertips where they can decide how and when they watch it. This challenges traditional avenues for brand engagement.

Ultimately, time is what brands are competing for when looking to engage with audiences and the key for brands to effectively do so when connecting to esports audiences is authenticity. Brands that have successfully done so have reaped the rewards such as adoration and loyalty from the audiences. However, authentically engaging with an esports audience requires an understanding of the microcultures that have developed in various esports titles. Which means brands must be able to understand the nuances of these microcultures to demonstrate authenticity when engaging.

Failure to do so leaves brands with ineffective campaigns or worse a backlash from the audience they're looking to engage with.

Brand engagement with their audience has evolved more in recent years. Authentic content marketing is a key component to successful campaigns for brands to reach the intended audience. For esports an increasing number of non-endemic brands have moved into the space as traditional digital and non-digital marketing channels are becoming less effective in reaching younger generations. The competition for brands to have the opportunity to engage with the esports audiences will only become fiercer in the coming years.

Cultural relevance of esports

Culture is evolving, with different pastimes and activities now driving youth engagement and popular culture. Meeting up with friends online has become the new normal, with esports being more than just competing in a video game. Socialising has been transported to virtual environments and has replaced clubs, festivals, shopping centres, and skatepark gatherings for many. We are seeing a convergence of entertainment cultures, where the worlds of gaming, music, film, entertainment, and fashion are coming together. We frame esports as a 'digital mediator' which offers a hub for these entities to co-exist in one virtual environment. This will be discussed in more detail later in this chapter, however critically this presents new consumption behaviours, socialisation opportunities, and expectations that need to be considered. For the younger generations these virtual domains bring together their passions in one space, and esports is the vehicle for them to engage, socialise, and connect with others who share a similar interest, as well as experience other forms of engagement, such as live concerts and non-gaming content which are appearing more frequently within esports environments.

We acknowledge that esports have been heavily associated with potential risks around addiction and sedentary behaviours, which will be discussed in further detail in a subsequent chapter; yet for many, esports act as a social connector. Virtual esports spaces bring together passionate, hyperconnected fans who are looking for dynamic, immersive experiences. Video game streaming platforms such as Twitch are enabling users to build online communities through heightened social engagement, and these digital spaces provide many with a sense of belonging, allowing the formation of social bonds and friendships (Trepte et al., 2012).

Esports communities offer a point of connection and camaraderie for gamers and play an important part of how individuals construct their personal identity. Esports participants are building their identity through hybrid environments, as socialisation, diverse experiences (game genres and content types range from violence and shooting to sport simulation), and interactions (avatars, instant messaging, social media, voice chat, LAN parties) are intersecting physical and virtual worlds (Xue et al., 2019). Further exemplifications of this are evident through the rapidly evolving technology that is resulting in mixed and full immersion media consumption. Virtual Reality (VR), Augmented Reality (AR), Mixed Reality (MR), and 360-degree video are all contributing to the next evolution of content, where consumers will be able to choose and engage with sport and entertainment content. Intel Sports is proposing compelling media experiences to sports fans through their 'Intel True View Platform', which is set to include VR experiences and will place fans in the middle of the action with varying degrees of immersive capabilities, from three degrees of freedom (3DoF) to six degrees of freedom (6DoF) immersive media experiences[1] (Gill & Kale, 2020).

This provides certain challenges for stakeholders and individuals who are not familiar with these digitalised spaces. Alongside brands and established industries who are now considering how to connect and resonate with digital natives through esports, for families, teachers, and parents the online gaming sphere offers a complex, virtual reality to navigate. Research by Meriläinen (2021) examined Finnish 16–19-year-old active gamers and noted a gaming-related generational gap between adolescents and their parents, which is influenced by parents' level of familiarity with gaming and esports. There was also a belief held by youth respondents that parents held negative stereotypes towards gaming. Esports is a cultural phenomenon embedded into the daily lives of today's younger generations especially, resulting in significant implications for family dynamics and parent-child interaction. Many families are having to navigate gaming cultures. Next, we present a case study of a Scottish Family with two children aged ten and eight, who are heavily involved in esports. This reflective piece provides a parental account of the role that esports plays in the culture and lifestyle of their family.

Case Study: Mum Vanessa[2] reflects on esports, family dynamics, and the realities of gaming culture.

We have 'Fortnite Fridays' in our house, it's not something as parents we would choose to do but it's a way of us spending time together . . . being involved with our kids in something they love rather than them sitting in their rooms with headphones on.

What is the esports culture in your home? Rebecca aged ten and Ethan aged eight play on different devices daily (Nintendo Switch and PlayStation), and their favourite game titles are mostly FIFA, Fortnite, and occasionally Rocket League. They both have 12-month subscriptions for PlayStation Plus and Nintendo Online. As well as the Fortnite Crew subscription for two accounts at £9.99 per month per subscription., which included the battle pass and 1000 vbucks to buy skins, weapons, or levels up.

We have a weekly Fortnite event, which we call Fortnite Friday just between us in the house, it's not something as parents we would choose to do on a Friday night, but it's a way of us spending time together, talking and being involved with our kids in something they love rather than them sitting in their rooms with headphones on. At Christmas and birthdays, you normally find that their main gifts normally revolve around whatever the "in" game is at that time. For example, Ethan's seventh birthday all he asked for was Fortnite merchandise and PlayStation vouchers so he could buy vbucks.

Why do they play? There was a definite increased use during lockdown for entertainment, social interaction, and communication with friends. They missed their friends a lot and all parents I had spoken to from their class actively encouraged them to play or get into games like Fortnite so they could keep in touch with their friends. Now we are out of lockdown, its more focused on the entertainment side as the social interaction and communication has increased in face-to-face contact. Their motives are different though, Ethan continues the social side with FIFA and competes with friends. Whereas Rebecca sets goals within the games and strives to complete them.

Do you have any concerns? Sometimes they are too focused on gaming rather than other things. Competitive gaming can affect, especially Rebecca's communication with us and friends as she zones out completely when playing. By this I mean if she is face to face with a friend who has come over to visit and that friend doesn't game, she would happily sit and play Fortnite and ignore her friend. Fortnite especially releases skins when you get to a certain level to entice you to keep playing, this can really have an effect because it's not only the game they are addicted to it's the ability to achieve the next level and reveal the skin. Ethan some-times finds the competitive side too much and can often become angry by bashing his controller on the desk or shouting at the TV which requires he be removed from the situation.

Reflections During lockdown the kids would play morning until night which I'm ashamed to admit but they were happy and with friends and there was literally nothing else to do. They were obsessed. However now the world is getting back to normal-ish, I'm glad to say that it's not as bad as before and some days they are straight on it after school or an hour and some days it's not mentioned at all and doesn't get played.

Esports presents a world with new dynamics, pressures, and forms of engagement for individuals and their families. The complexity of the esports industry, in terms of different subscriptions, gaming modes and 'trending' game titles can create a dynamic environment that challenges gaming literacy and optimal management of healthy engagement with gaming for parents and individuals. Yet, the above case study also provides an example of how esports can be encouraged and incorporated into family culture.

Esports stakeholders

The digital and contemporary nature of esports means that multiple stake-holders were involved in the creation and subsequent sustainability of the industry. A diverse range of actors are interdependent and reliant on each other to ensure the effective functioning of the esports sector, due to its complex and digitalised form. Table 1.1 outlines the primary stakeholders within the industry, which is fundamentally underpinned by commercial business models and ownership structures. Game developers and publish-ers (i.e., EA Sports, Valve Corporation, Riot Games) own the intellectual property of video games, which changes the very nature and dynamic of the environment, as the whole industry is anchored through the publish-ers and the game titles they have developed. This has led to the fractured, ungoverned nature of the industry that can be observed today, as esports was unconstrained by traditional forms of governance that regulates other industries.

Table 1.1 Core stakeholder groups of the esports industry

Stakeholder Groups	Examples	Definition
Game Publishers and Developers	EA Sports Tencent Games Sony Interactive Entertainment Riot Games Inc Valve Corporation Activision Blizzard	Developers are the organisations that have created the video games and game publishers own the intellectual property of video games.
Players	Johan Sundstein (aka N0tail) Lasse Urpalainen (aka Matumbaman) Lee Sang-hyeok (aka Faker) Andreas Højsleth (aka Xyp9x) Sasha Hostyn (aka Scarlett)	Athletes or individuals that can compete at either an amateur or semi-professional or professional level. This could be competing as an individual or as part of a team.
Fans		Fans are individuals that follow specific esports titles, leagues, and teams; as well as spectating they often participate themselves (either in the same title or different esports genres).
Leagues	Call of Duty League FIFA 21 Global Series The National Association of Collegiate Esports (NACE) NBA 2K	The competitive structure in which tournaments and events are organised. Globally there are established Leagues (tier 1) and then emerging lower-level Leagues, as well as collegiate Leagues. In many cases certain Leagues result in points or places available for teams to compete in the global title championship.
Teams and Franchises	Excel Esports Fanatic Team Liquid Ninjas in Pyjamas Team Dignitas Cloud9	A group of players who have been selected as members of a team and then will compete in specific esports leagues and tournaments.
Major Tournaments and Event Organisers	Dreamhack The International ESL	Groups and organisations that are responsible for organising and hosting esports events and tournaments.

Stakeholder Groups	Examples	Definition
Media: Broadcast and Streaming Platforms	Twitch YouTube Gaming Twitter	This could include traditional broadcasters who now offer a range of media and streaming services. Also, there are specific organisations that have been created to provide online media and streaming platforms for users and fans.
Federations and Associations	International *Esports* Federation (IESF) British Esports Association World Esports Association (WESA)	The organisations that are responsible for the development, legitimisation, and regulatory structures within esports. These are often non-profit organisations who act as governing bodies, yet in many cases have limited control or power within the industry, but rather act as influencing bodies to try and create, encourage, or change regulation.
Sponsors	Mercedes Intel Red bull DHL Monster Anda Seat	Both endemic and non-endemic brands are involved in investing in the esports industry. In return for access to rights, they are aiming to achieve specific objectives relevant to their brand strategy. Sponsorship can occur at multiple levels of the esports environment, for example the sponsorship of specific tournaments, teams, leagues, or through the endorsement of esports athletes themselves.

Is esports a sport? Does it matter?

Esports, its definition, and more specifically esports' position within the mainstream sporting policy and governance landscape is highly contested. Within scholarly research, esports has challenged the traditional notion of sport. Existing distinctions between play, games, and sport have resulted in the identification of key characteristics that help classify a sport, such as whether the activity is structured, competitive in nature, and culturally positioned (Jenny et al., 2017). However, it is the level of physicality and effective governance, which is usually the area of contestation.

Esports requires both physical (such as speed of movement, dexterity, fine motor skills) and cognitive skills (including strategic thinking, visuospatial memory, attention, perception, and information processing). Yet, all definitions to date have not accounted for the dependency of the numerous physical attributes, which dictate athletic performance and outcomes. The physical demands and performance characteristics of esports have been acknowledged, with Carter and Gibbs (2013) reflecting on previous work which advocated for the athleticism and professionalism of esports noted that "eSport is a physically draining, expertise driven activity which hinges on performance in both the physical and digital domains. Any conceptualization that eSports are a fully virtual performance is false" (p. 2). Despite increased commercial engagement, academic discourse regarding the classification of esports inherently questions whether it can be defined as a sport (Heere, 2018; Holden et al., 2017; Jonasson & Thiborg, 2010). Yet, Holden et al. (2017) recognises the wider implications surrounding the positioning and role of esports, and its acknowledgment as a sport (or not), that are critical to the reputational, policy, and integrity implications of sport business, as discussed further in Chapter 2. Given the popularity, success, and importance of esports within today's popular culture, does esports need to fit the traditional notion of sport? More importantly, the focus should be on how the sports industry is adapting to global changes and shifts in technology, connectivity, and consumption habits, which are redefining how we conceptualise sport.

Esports are a contemporary phenomenon characterised as unique, immersive, and global in nature. Participation and spectatorship with esports are not limited by geographical boundaries, and it is possible for individuals to engage from anywhere in the world. It is only through the competition structures that a more localised approach occurs, with Leagues and tournaments based within specific global contexts (for example, North American or European Leagues). Converse to most other industries which are shifting from offline to online, most esports activity happens online and is transitioning to offline activities, through tournaments, events, and physical interactions.

Esports is distinctive in the way it can be consumed, compared with the traditional sport, entertainment, and media industries. There are numerous ways to engage with esports, whether as a gamer (participating), as an observer (watching officially or through an alternative stream), as a creator (as a streamer, castor), as well as through interactions and exchanges on other social; platforms (Reddit, Discord, Twitter), which are often home to online esports communities. Importantly, this signals a change more broadly within the sports industry, as especially post COVID-19, we are seeing a shifting focus toward digital spaces and virtual fan engagement, which will be discussed in Chapter 5, as we see sports increasingly diversi-fying into esports.

Existing consumption models and established norms around content types that are traditionally associated with the media and entertainment industries are dissolving, as social media and live streaming platforms such as Tik Tok, Twitch, Twitter, and YouTube Gaming are enabling consumers to simultaneously create, consume, and engage with content. Therefore, in a global, digitalised world where consumers have technology integrated into their everyday lives, they expect fluid, immersive engagement across other entertainment and leisure spheres as well. Therefore, regardless of whether esports fits into the narrow, historical parameters which once defined sport, esports provide a virtual environment rich with potential for collaboration and convergence between different industries, which until recently have only existed in silos.

Esports acting as a digital mediator

The digital, dynamic, and innovative nature of esports, coupled with its global reach and popularity is resulting in its use as a 'digital media-tor' (Hayday & Collison, Forthcoming). Specifically, esports spaces are being leveraged by other industries with collaborations being evidenced across the spheres of entertainment, sport, music, media, and fashion (see Figure 1.1). Esports is acting as a digital platform, meaning its purpose and function extends beyond being the home for competitive gaming. Specifi-cally, for the first time we are seeing a convergence of industries, initiated in online esports environments, yet resulting in opportunities and impli-cations offline as well (for example fashion brand Louis Vuitton creating skins for an avatar in League of Legends online, resulted in the creation of related merchandise such as t-shirts, luggage tags, and accessories that can be purchased offline).

Virtual esports game environments offer a unique means to connect with digital consumers through memorable experiences, allowing brands and organisations to engage and ultimately monetise these audiences. Through multiple examples given next, we outline how esports is being utilised as a site of convergence and collaboration between multiple industries.

Global franchises such as Fortnite[3] and Marvel collaborated in 2018 on a special crossover mode in Fortnite Battle Royale, to promote the blockbuster movie "Avengers: Infinity War", which starred the movie's villain Thanos in the game (Webster, 2018). The film industry giants saw an opportunity to promote the new Avengers movie by embedding their characters into a new virtual domain (Fortnite), which has millions of global users. This offered access to new and existing audiences, but importantly provides a novel and

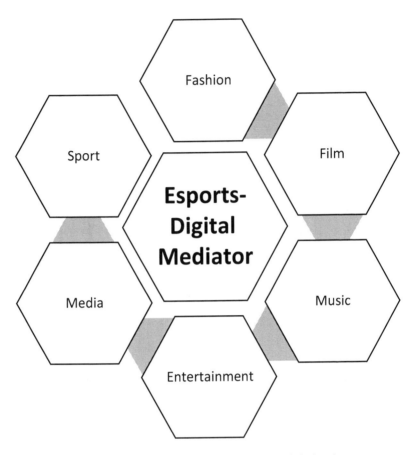

Figure 1.1 Esports as a digital mediator converging multiple industries

creative consumer experience. Within the music industry, Spotify has partnered with Riot Games making them the exclusive audio-streaming partner for League of Legends' (LoL) global events, a dedicated LoL hub will be set up on Spotify offering collection of music, podcasts, and playlists, all associated with the game (Dredge, 2020).

Further musical collaborations have been seen within game titles. For example, in Fortnite live virtual concerts have been hosted within the game environment. In 2019, DJ Marshmello hosted a live concert complete with dancing avatars and impressive visual effects which was attended by 10.7 million users (Webster, 2019). During the COVID-19 pandemic, rapper Travis Scott collaborated with Epic Games and hosted five concerts within Fortnite, which allowed users to co-create an immersive and interactive experience, through bespoke Scott-related skins that could be collected for users' own avatars, along with users being able to hold flaming microphones up during the concert itself (Stuart, 2020). The O2 Arena and Universal Studios are now getting in on the act, with a virtual recreation of the London music venue being placed within Fortnite's creative mode. Easy Life, a UK band, hosted a virtual concert in June 2021, which offered exclusive items and secret rooms to explore inspired by the band's lyrics (Teixeira, 2021).

Luxury fashion companies Louis Vuitton and Balenciaga are brands that typically wouldn't be associated with the esports sector, however online gaming spaces could be seen as the new playground for the fashion labels and brands. One of the most iconic partnerships between the worlds of fashion and esports came in the form of Louis Vuitton collaboration with Riot Games. Specifically focused on League of Legends, they created in-game prestige skins for characters, designed the trophy case for the 2019 World Championship and created a capsule collection and products in tribute to Qiyana, a female protagonist within the game (Biondi, 2020). Balenciaga will debut its fall clothing collection in a videogame called Afterworld: The Age of Tomorrow, which has been created to provide a gamified, immersive experience for users, with tasks and interactions split across five levels (Porter, 2020). Starting in a Balenciaga store, this game will take individuals through an adventure based around human destiny, which culminates in a virtual rave (Porter, 2020). At a time when large scale fashion shows and launches are not always possible, due to the COVID-19 pandemic, innovation is needed. Some fashion houses have looked to live streaming to promote their fashion lines online, yet this specific focus on a futuristic computer role playing game, showcases the potential of esports spaces (Natividad, 2021).

Recognition and involvement of such global fashion brands not only cements the cultural relevance and recognition of esports, but also highlights the value of specific online communities that express fandom towards a specific game title, team, player, or character. Brands (through collaborations and partnerships) can build a relationship with specific esports communities, allowing them to create brand affinity, influence purchasing decisions and develop brand trust. We are in effect, seeing the norms and traditional ways of marketing and communicating with consumers being re-defined, as esports virtual and cultural characteristics are now being leveraged and offer a digital vehicle to support collaboration between multiple industries.

The convergence of industries that until recently have been siloed, offers esports organisations a distinct opportunity as a digital mediator to create powerful, unique experiences for consumers through the virtual environments and online communities they have created. Moreover, the loyalty and subscription models associated with many gaming brands can be leveraged to create enhanced brand equity through loyalty and brand buzz (word of mouth) and engagement. Although there were examples of such inter-industry collaboration before the COVID-19, the pandemic has accelerated the need for organisations to have a presence in a digital environment. The ever-digitalised world has resulted in modes of consumption shifting, and consumers want to be part of an immersive, interactive experience that is at least in part digitally driven.

Conclusion

Dynamic, complex, and innovative are key characteristics of the esports industry, and as a fast-paced, dynamic industry, there is a myriad of opportunities that can be explored for marketers and publishers. Critically, we are seeing growth both in terms of participation and commercial outcomes, alongside the entry of new stakeholders at an unprecedented rate. The creative and entrepreneurial cultural foundations of esports will translate to further investment and mainstream acceptance, providing strong potential for esports as a multi-industry virtual connector beyond gaming. With the velocity of growth of the sector, it is critical that the governance and regulatory structures evolve to mitigate risk, protect vulnerable young participants, and forge trust in esports. Given the nascent state of governance across the sector, the next chapter discusses the challenges of governance in esports, the risks, and outlines some of the regulatory structures and models that are emerging within the esports sector.

Notes

1 Degrees of Freedom (DoF) refer to the number of ways a rigid object can move through 3D space. There are six total degrees of freedom based around a rotational and translational movement around the x, y, and z axes. VR devices and equipment are generally 3DoF or 6DoF (Google VR, 2018).
2 Pseudonyms have been provided to protect the identity of the family and children.
3 A battle royale shooter game released by Epic Games in 2017.

References

Biondi, A. (2020, August 28). Fashion's new playground: Esports and gaming. *Vogue Business*. www.voguebusiness.com/technology/fashion-esports-gaming-monetisation

Carter, M., & Gibbs, M. (2013). eSports in EVE online: Skullduggery, fair play and acceptability in an unbounded competition. In *Proceedings of the 8th international conference on the foundations of digital games* (pp. 47–54). SASDG.

Cranmer, E. E., Han, D. I. D., van Gisbergen, M., & Jung, T. (2021). Esports matrix: Structuring the esports research agenda. *Computers in Human Behavior, 117*, 1–13. https://doi.org/10.1016/j.chb.2020.106671

Dredge, S. (2020, August 25). Spotify's first esports partnership is with Riot Games. *Music Ally*. https://musically.com/2020/08/25/spotifys-first-esports-partnership-is-with-riot-games/

Funk, D. C., Pizzo, A. D., & Baker, B. J. (2018). eSport management: Embracing eSport education and research opportunities. *Sport Management Review, 21*(1), 7–13. https://doi.org/10.1016/j.smr.2017.07.008

Gill, H., & Kale, R. (2020, November 16). SVG tech insight: Immersive media experiences with intel true view delivers new reality for sports. *Sport Video Group Blog*. www.sportsvideo.org/2020/11/16/svg-tech-insight-immersive-media-experiences-with-intel-true-view-delivers-new-reality-for-sports/

Google VR. (2018, September 21). Degrees of freedom. *Google VR*. https://developers.google.com/vr/discover/degrees-of-freedom

Hayday, E. J., & Collison, H. (Forthcoming). Esport: Digital mediation in a restricted world. In S. Frawley & N. Schulenkorf (Eds.), *Routledge handbook for sport and COVID-19*. Routledge.

Heere, B. (2018). Embracing the sportification of society: Defining e-sports through a polymorphic view on sport. *Sport Management Review, 21*(1), 21–24. https://doi.org/10.1016/j.smr.2017.07.002

Holden, J. T., Kaburakis, A., & Rodenberg, R. (2017). The future is now: Esports policy considerations and potential litigation. *Journal of Legal Aspects Sport, 27*, 46–78. doi:10.1123/jlas.2016–0018

Jenny, S. E., Manning, R. D., Keiper, M. C., & Olrich, T. W. (2017). Virtual (ly) athletes: Where eSports fit within the definition of "Sport". *Quest, 69*(1), 1–18. https://doi.org/10.1080/00336297.2016.1144517

Jonasson, K., & Thiborg, J. (2010). Electronic sport and its impact on future sport. *Sport in Society, 13*(2), 287–299. https://doi.org/10.1080/17430430903522996

King, D., & Delfabbro, P. (2019). Video game monetization (e.g., 'loot boxes'): A blueprint for practical social responsibility measures. *International Journal of Mental Health and Addiction, 17*, 166–179. http://doi.org/10.1007/s11469-018-0009-3

Meriläinen, M. (2021). Crooked views and relaxed rules: How teenage boys experience parents' handling of digital gaming. *Media, and Communication, 9*(1), 62–72. https://doi.org/10.17645/mac.v9i1.3193

Natividad, A. (2021, January 11). Balenciaga released its fall 2021 collection inside a futuristic RPG-style video game. *Muse*. https://musebycl.io/gaming/balenciaga-released-its-fall-2021-collection-inside-a-futuristic-rpg-style-video-game

Newzoo. (2021, March 9). Global esports & live streaming market report. *Newzoo*. https://newzoo.com/insights/trend-reports/newzoos-global-esports-live-streaming-market-report-2021-free-version/

Peng, Q., Dickson, G., Scelles, N., Grix, J., & Brannagan, P. M. (2020). Esports governance: Exploring stakeholder dynamics. *Sustainability*, *12*(19), 8270. https://doi.org/10.3390/su12198270

Porter, J. (2020, November 26). Balenciaga made a video game to debut its next clothing collection. *The Verge*. www.theverge.com/2020/11/26/21721371/balenciaga-afterworld-the-age-of-tomorrow-fashion-launch-video-game

Scholz, T. M. (2020). Deciphering the world of esports. *International Journal on Media Management*, *22*, 1–12. https://doi.org/10.1080/14241277.2020.1757808

Stuart, K. (2020, April 24). More than 12m players watch Travis Scott concert in Fortnite. *The Guardian*. www.theguardian.com/games/2020/apr/24/travis-scott-concert-fortnite-more-than-12m-players-watch

Teixeira, M. (2021, June 21). O2 "supervenue" launches in 'Fortnite' for interactive virtual gig experience. *NME*. www.nme.com/news/gaming-news/o2-supervenue-launches-in-fortnite-for-interactive-virtual-gig-experience-2974033

Thompson, H. (2020, January 9). How Fortnite changed online gaming forever. *Nerd Stash*. https://thenerdstash.com/how-fortnite-changed-online-gaming-forever/?nowprocket=1

Trepte, S., Reinecke, L., & Juechems, K. (2012). The social side of gaming: How playing online computer games creates online and offline social support. *Computers in Human Behavior*, *28*, 832–839. https://doi.org/10.1016/j.chb.2011.12.003

Wagner, M. (2006). On the scientific relevance of eSport. In J. Arreymbi, V. A. Clincy, O. L. Droegehorn, S. Joan, M. G. Ashu, J. A. Ware, S. Zabir, & H. R. Arabnia (Eds.), *Proceedings of the 2006 international conference on internet computing and conference on computer game development* (pp. 437–440). CSREA Press.

Webster, A. (2018, May 7). Thanos is coming to Fortnite for a limited time. *The Verge*. www.theverge.com/2018/5/7/17326678/fortnite-avengers-crossover-thanos

Webster, A. (2019, February 21). Fortnite's Marshmello concert was the game's biggest event ever. *The Verge*. www.theverge.com/2019/2/21/18234980/fortnite-marshmello-concert-viewer-numbers

Xue, H., Newman, J. I., & Du, J. (2019). Narratives, identity, and community in esports. *Leisure Studies*, *38*(6), 845–861. https://doi.org/10.1080/02614367.2019.1640778

2 Esports governance and regulation

Key Questions

1. *Why is governance needed in esports and what are the key regulatory issues?*
2. *What are the challenges for effective governance in esports?*
3. *What are the esports governance models currently and are they working?*

Governance in esports: is it the wild west?

The future of sport is contingent upon effective governance, but traditional governance models associated with sport need to evolve to meet the unique challenges and complexity of esports. The new culture of independence, creativity, entrepreneurship, and anti-authoritarianism is evident among next generations and the esports sector presents opportunities to reimagine effective governance and the positive growth of esports. The commercial, digitalised, and networked nature of the esports sector is unique and exponentially growing, as highlighted in the previous chapter. Esports have emerged as a preferred recreational, competitive, and even professional pastime, merging entertainment with sport. As discussed in Chapter 1, the uniquely popular and digital nature of esports have evolved them to be a digital mediator, converging fashion, sport, music, and media. There is evidence to suggest that esports rival live sports, cinema, and music, as the most popular form of content among next generation consumers, who participate through playing and streaming across hyperconnected events and platforms such as Twitch and YouTube, (Jang et al., 2020). Esports are also consumed for longer periods of time and are engaged with more frequently than traditional forms of entertainment, particularly among young audiences, and therefore represent a very attractive commercial opportunity (Jang et al., 2020).

DOI: 10.4324/9781003213598-2

Governance and regulation of this burgeoning sector have not aligned with the dramatic growth and unique landscape that has emerged. Unlike traditional sports, which are not owned, but rather federated or regulated by external entities, esports are entirely digital, privately owned by gaming publishers, and self-regulated. This chapter outlines the governance challenges faced by esports and advocates the need for some protectionist governance for esports participants, but equally to ensure the positive growth of the sector. Current trust in the esports industry and growth is challenged by the lack of governance, and by addressing this issue, more sophisticated ownership and investment models can be supported. While the sector is rapidly evolving, it is important to consider its role in the broader global sports and entertainment landscape in shaping next generations' socio-cultural development. It is also important to recognise that governance in this domain is a dynamic process. Optimal governance for esports may differ from the patchwork of governing bodies traditionally associated with traditional sport, and esports does present an opportunity to establish new models of active governance (Scholz, 2019).

The importance of esports governance

Anecdotal reports suggest that esports are the "wild west" of governance, whether considered entertainment, sport, or a hybrid of these (Scholz, 2019). In essence, the esports sector has been founded as digital, global, and agile, providing both new challenges and opportunities for the sector to influence and govern effectively. Challenges are amplified by the lack of consistent governance and regulation within the sector, the uniquely commercially driven, digital foundation of the sector, and the youth-centric consumer base (Chao, 2017). The combination of federations and governance bodies that typically govern traditional sports are increasingly unable to address the rapidly changing media, culture, and consumption landscape associated with esports. The popularity of esports, its digital platform, and private ownership render it a new domain through which to build governance priorities. While the private intellectual property ownership of esports will always separate it from the social, amateur roots of traditional sport, the governance problems experienced by the ecosystem from tournament organisers to leagues and teams mirror traditional sports to some extent, but diverge in some areas, related to the digital nature of the participation.

The current state of esports is that it is a largely self-regulated industry, with some publishers developing compulsory codes of conduct and policies, in relation to cheating, player contracts, anti-doping, and arbitration. In some jurisdictions, legislative intervention or codified norms have been introduced in response to policy concerns in relation to infiltration of organised crime, illegal betting, and the need to protect vulnerable minors (Kelly et al., 2021). The emergence of not-for-profit organisations such as the Esports Integrity Commission aligns with increasing acknowledgement of corruption risk in esports. The Commission positions itself as an independent integrity safeguarding organisation for esports, with particular focus upon match fixing and doping, but only has jurisdiction to signatory members (Czegledy, 2021). While these initiatives are a positive step, the issue with this fragmented current state of governance is that there is no consistency of codes or policies and sanctioning for non-compliance across the esports industry.

There is evidence that the esports industry acknowledges a need for improved governance (Windholz, 2020), but the optimal governance approach is less clear, with options ranging from self-regulation to independent, universal governance, or a hybrid of the two (Peng et al., 2020). An absence of effective governance in the industry poses trust and reputational risk which will threaten the continued growth and commercialisation of the sector, and potentially other sectors with which it is becoming associated, such as Sport for Development (SfD) or diplomacy. Without predicable and effective governance structures, esports will be perceived as too risky as a vehicle or partner for brands, governments, or sports. More importantly, safeguarding of minors in esports is clearly a priority, yet with an absence of consistent oversight, the rapidly evolving digital context, and lack of independent scrutiny and supportive structures, governance issues remain. However, the private ownership of esports also represents an opportunity for new and effective governance in the sector, given that many private companies will demand high standards of compliance, in addition to good citizenship.

Motivation for enhanced governance structures across the esports ecosystem also stems from the need to comply with conventions protecting children, including the United Nations Convention on the Rights of the Child and European Convention on Human Rights, and the associated scrutiny relating to any transgression of these conventions across sport (Davey & Lundy, 2011). This compliance is not only worthy of ethical pursuit, but also reputationally and commercially, presumably with sponsors, investors, and ambassadors demanding safeguarding of minor participants. The global nature of esports also renders it a viable diplomatic and socially responsible platform which must establish robust governance to realise such positive potential. However, the mapping of complex interrelationships, power structures, and interaction with traditional sports required to implement esports' governance is challenging. Traditional sports have taught us that governance must be a dynamic process to remain relevant to changes in sports science, digitisation, commercialisation, risk, and consumption.

Esports therefore is likely to require innovative governance solutions that align with esports' contemporary nature.

Esports as a sport: governance implications

One of the motivations for the industry to embrace more effective governance is that to fully realise both commercial and mainstream potential, it must be recognised as a sport through global organisations such as the International Olympic Committee (Hallmann & Giel, 2018). Preparing for a bid to enter the Olympic schedule requires a reinforcement of structure, alignment across the ecosystem, and trust that can lead to receipt of significant funding and development of the sport. Another advantage of a sports status would enable esports to be brought under the jurisdiction of existing legislation and codes, such as the Court of Arbitration for Sport, the World Anti-Doping Code, The Olympic Charter, criminal, anti-discrimination, and anti-gambling legislation. To qualify as a sport, the weight of literature and practice suggest that popularity, intense competition, commercialisation, and robust governance are critical (Hallman & Giel, 2018). Esports are clearly aligned with the first three criteria, but governance represents a challenge. The motivation to integrate suitable governance into esports is therefore critical to understand and implement across the complex esports ecosystem, including publishers, participants, media, sponsors, team owners, and tournament/league owners. The very distinct characteristics across different games, leagues, and genres, and their short-lived popularity add additional layers of complexity to governance. Esports can be analogised to the Summer Olympics, except with a greater diversity of sports. The complexity of interactions in the system means that a diversity of perspectives is needed to inform the governance of the sector, rather than a top-down approach.

Many sports are already embracing esports as part of their business sustainability and diversification and brand extension strategies, aimed at resonating with next generation fans. For example, Formula One and e-racing, FIFA World Cup, [Team Liquid, Fnatic, Splyce, organisations such as Origen, Misfits Gaming, and Excel Esports (Hayward, 2019). This diversification strategy by traditional sports has impacted esports governance models by transferring traditional sports governance models into the esports realm. While the esports sector has endeavoured to lead its own governance mechanisms against a backdrop of a dearth of policy enforcement mechanisms, these efforts have been inconsistently applied, and not universally adopted. For example, players banned from a tournament for breach of relevant codes may transfer to another esports tournament or team, due to the regulatory scope only extending to competition participants. For example,

Team Newbee have been issued a lifetime ban from Chinese competitions for match fixing, but this does not stop them from playing in our leagues or competitive game titles (Stubbs, 2020). Governance issues such as these are discussed in more detail in the next section.

Governance and legal issues

While many problems associated with traditional sports are mirrored in esports, the vulnerabilities in esports are different. Esports' unique attributes create specific governance challenges, including safeguarding of its extensive market of minors, balancing rights of commercial owners of the sector and the complexity of consistent, cross-jurisdictional enforcement. Moreover, the digital nature of esports incentivises unique approaches to betting-related fixing, cheating, and online bullying such as manipulation of gaming coding and structure, ability to information-share in real time, and in-game mechanics (Funk et al., 2018). Market power vested through monopolisation of intellectual property ownership by game publishers also acts as a barrier to external regulation and governance, and places stronger emphasis upon effective self-regulatory mechanisms. Consequently, the growing commercialisation of esports has been accompanied by increased integrity issues including match fixing, doping, and illegal gambling, harmful product advertising and safeguarding of players, and related calls for increased regulation and governance (Ghoshal, 2019; Hollist, 2015; Macey et al., 2020). The establishment of the Esports Integrity Commission in 2015 with offices in the United Kingdom and Australia is testament to the integrity challenges now endemic in esports, and several other international and national organisations have been established aimed at improving governance and mitigating risks across the sector, with varying degrees of success, as outlined in the next section.

Esports' unique virtual position enables novel forms of integrity transgression, such as e-doping and information sharing through hyperconnected networks, imply a need for esports-specific governance codes and policy. While current governance and regulatory models associated with sport such as the World Anti-Doping Code are useful frameworks, esports require customised policy contingent upon its wide-ranging stakeholder support and active participation in governance. In addition to its digital nature, the diversity of esports games, genres, competitions, and jurisdictions in which they are played and streamed, adds to the complexity of effective governance and consistent policy for the sector. Some governments have introduced regulation in response to integrity risk. For instance, the US currently has several regulations in place (e.g., Wire Act, 1961 and the Unlawful Internet Gambling Enforcement Act, 2006). However, in other jurisdictions such as

India, uncertainty of gambling definitions means that regulation of esports betting, particularly in relation to novel forms such as microtransactions in game, is challenging (Ghoshal, 2019). The key governance issues currently experienced in esports are outlined in the next section. With so many young esports participants and limited consistency of governance, player welfare and contracting have been particularly challenging.

Labour issues

As a burgeoning employment sector, esports is increasingly challenged by disputes relating to player contracting and wellbeing (Holden & Baker, 2019). Key reasons for these challenges include issues relating to minors as employees and contractors, and a lack of consistent protections and rights afforded to employees. For example, three of the largest and most lucrative esports leagues, League of Legends Championship Series, Electronic Sports League (ESL), and The International have different employment contract approaches. The main driver of employee contract issues in esports is the market power of publishers with their exclusive intellectual property ownership, and the resulting unequal power between publishers or tournament owners and players in contractual negotiations (Kelly et al., 2021; Wong, 2020). This has resulted in exclusion of third parties from hosting or participating if they are not affiliated with the publishers' intellectual property in some instances (Windholz, 2020). For example, Activision demonstrated reluctance to grant tournament licences to third party Overwatch event organisers and there have been reports of similar practices by publishers across other tournaments (Intergalactic Gaming, 2019).

In any event, the short esports career duration disincentivises players from forming a union, and licensees and participants are threatened with immediate revocation by powerful publishers for non-compliance with publisher guidelines, often without a right of independent appeal (Windholz, 2020). Player exploitation is therefore a key integrity risk in esports, stemming from a combination of market power vested in publishers, and the relative inexperience of youth employees. While some independent governance organisations have emerged in response to these issues and described in more detail in the next section, these entities have suffered legitimacy issues from different esports stakeholders due to lack of enforcement powers and inconsistency across the esports ecosystem (Johri, 2020).

Micro transactions in game

The integration of virtual purchases or microtransactions in games is a common strategy to promote engagement and sometimes also to raise esports competition prize money. Loot boxes and skins are commonly used to incentivise game participants with game-changing items, and experts warn of the likeness of these transactions with gambling due to the randomness of the loot box contents combined with the anticipation of winning, and resulting potential for psychological and financial risk and, at worst, gaming addiction (King & Delfabbro 2019; Li et al., 2019; Browne, 2020).

There is currently no consensus as to how loot boxes and other types of microtransactions in online video gaming should be regulated, with some jurisdictions regulating microtransactions specifically (e.g., China, United States, and Korea) and others relying upon existing anti-gambling legislation alignment (e.g., United Kingdom, New Zealand, Canada, Sweden, and France) (Drummond & Sauer, 2018). Some governments, such as China and Korea, have regulated microtransactions in-game for minors, capped expenditure, and require more transparency through warnings on gaming packaging, and in-game, and incentivised self- regulation of the industry through tax relief and funding (Xiao & Henderson, 2019). Self-regulation is emerging as one model to address the challenges within the industry, taking a socially responsible approach to limit the likelihood of players overspending by capping microtransaction expenditure for individual players and changing game design, purchase system features, and ensuring transparency to ensure consumers and parents are fully informed (King & Delfabbro, 2019). Examples of current measures exhibited by publishers include the ability for players to set limits on their loot box spending, the removal of items which confer a competitive advantage on winners, a ban on loot box solicitation and scarcity offers, a requirement for games to display the odds of winning, and age restrictions for games incorporating loot boxes (King & Delfabbro, 2019).

Player welfare and social issues

Misconduct in esports has been escalating, with reported incidents and legal redress sought in relation to racial vilification and bullying, harassment, and cheating. Many of these issues are sparked by the digital nature of esports, and heavy use of social media and concurrent communications during play among the young demographic of both players and streamers. While esports organisations in many cases have established relevant policies and codes of conduct, absence of a single, independent governing body renders enforcement and jurisdiction challenging.

An example of this is with market power issues. In 2013, for instance, Riot Games was criticised for modifying its contract terms to prevent players from participating in other competitions and from streaming their playing of other video games (Chao, 2017). In 2016, Riot Games faced criticism after banning three teams, Renegades Team, Team Impulse, and Team Dragon Knights from the League of Legends Championship Series without any recourse for appeal (Wolf, 2016). Additional practices, including uncensored social media use by participants typically adopting pseudonyms and regularly engaging in rumour and speculation without scrutiny and accountability is a key problem. The practice of team housing also increases risk to player welfare, with team owners encouraging teams to live and train together, without safeguarding player welfare in terms of team dynamics, doping, diet, and hours of training (Wong, 2020).

The current lack of gender diversity across esports is also an issue, with many reports of sexual harassment, discrimination, and bullying of female players (Darvin et al., 2020). The relative youth and inexperience of players also disadvantages them in contractual negotiations, leaving them vulnerable to financial exploitation and inadequately safeguarded in many instances. Many esports coaches, team owners, and league administrators are themselves young and inexperienced, with limited understanding of appropriate governance and conduct, compounding the risk for player welfare. In the event of a complaint, players are often only left with avenues of reporting the complaint to publishers or leagues, many of which also own the teams. This represents a conflict of interest and potential for bias, with prosecutor, defendant, and judge being the same entity.

Moreover, rights of independent appeal or investigation are not typically provided in the self-regulated system, again leaving players rights largely unprotected (Windholz, 2020; Kelly et al., 2021). This was the case in the Tainted Minds Scandal where living arrangements and conditions were seen as unsuitable by the players, manager, and coach, and lacking some basic rights outlined in the contracts between the parties (Goslin, 2017). Organisations such as the Esports Integrity Coalition and inclusion of some rights to external arbitration by larger publishers such as Riot and Valve are positive mechanisms which will hopefully be replicated and supported across the industry (Brickell, 2017).

Doping

As with all competitive sports, doping has been found to be used in esports for performance enhancing purposes, famously by admission of the Cloud9 team in 2015 (Graham, 2015) following winning $250,000 USD in a major tournament. Drugs including Adderall, Ritalin, and Selegiline are known to enhance alertness, energy, concentration, and reaction times. Substances such as these have been used by esports players, and many publishers and event organisers have developed anti-doping policies in codes of conduct in an effort to mitigate doping. Drug testing during tournaments is also being implemented in many cases, such as within the eFIFA World Cup and ESL, but unfortunately anti-doping policy and practice is not consistently implemented across esports. Practices of housing teams together for training, the addictive nature of gaming structures, and lack of mitigation through oversight and regulation relating to gaming hours, incentivise the use of drugs to boost alertness, reaction time, and energy. While some of these drugs are regarded as performance enhancing and therefore classified as cheating under some codes, the protection of minors' and young players' wellbeing is also a concern.

Match fixing, e-doping, and corruption

The illegal and legal betting markets for esports are estimated to exceed $250 billion USD, according to Sportsradar, and the sector attracts many established betting agencies and bookmakers, including an esports specialist betting entity, Unikrn, Activision and some of the publishers are collaborating with Sportradar and crime agencies to enhance monitoring and detection of match fixing and corruption incentivised by the lucrative betting markets associated with esports, including League of Legends, CO: GO, Dota 2, FIFA 21, and Call of Duty (Sporttechie, 2020).

Teams and athletes can engage in cheating by leveraging and interfering with the software and equipment supporting the competitions, known as e-doping. For example, cheat software can be installed, or systems hacked aimed at opponents' devices to gain an advantage. Cheating software cases have included slowing down systems of opponents, enabling superior vision, and prevention of reloading weapons (Conroy et al., 2021). Publishers and Leagues regularly ban players engaging in e-doping and match fixing, and these bans are published and can result in a lifetime ban. However, many banned players establish new accounts and participate in alternative Leagues, due to the inconsistency of universal governance structures.

Match fixing is one of the largest integrity challenges in esports and continues to proliferate due to the current lack of holistic governance and decentralised nature of the industry. Reports of alleged fixing and corruption are pervasive and there have been several cases involving law enforcement, as well as internal intervention by publishers and event organisers. For example, several players affiliated with organised crime linked to an illegal betting syndicate were arrested in Korea for match fixing in StarCraft2, in 2015, and evidence suggests teams have been established specifically for match fixing purposes (Mitchell, 2014). The Akuma match fixing case in 2021, detailed in case study (Box 2.1) demonstrates that esports integrity needs to be addressed in a more cohesive and effective way across the ecosystem.

Case Study: Akuma Cheating Scandal

The CS: GO Majors hosted 16 teams in May 2021. Akuma's team consisted of a relatively new group of players. The team came third in the competition, netting $5,000 in prize money and 1,400 Regional Major Rankings ("RMR") points. RMR points are allocated to teams and players based upon performance and determine qualification to the Major. However, it was alleged Akuma cheated to gain a competitive edge by using radar hacks and external aim locks. There was also a suggestion that the team had been in contact with tournament staff. Decisions were made during the tournament to disable the anti-cheat software and there was no record of TeamSpeak (the mechanism by which players communicate with each other while in action). It is uncertain why these decisions were made. RESF investigated Akuma on May 30, concluding that there was no evidence of cheating and the tournament had not been compromised. The Russian Esports Federation's ("RESF") investigation was criticised by 14 of the 16 teams involved in the competition who wrote to Valve asking for a full investigation into Akuma's play. The teams criticised the RESF's lack of available anti-cheating measures to allow the investigation to proceed. ESIC concluded potential match fixing or betting fraud behaviour had occurred, but because the regulator had no jurisdiction over the competition, the only mechanism was to refer this case to Valve. The implementation and oversight of anti-cheating procedures could have potentially prevented this incident. This case highlights the need for greater powers for ESIC to regulate to maintain the confidence and goodwill of stakeholders as esports continues to build momentum. The integrity of the regulatory processes is a crucial component of building the sustainability of esports (Kozelco, 2021).

Several publishers and Leagues have introduced specific codes of conduct and regulations aimed at preventing cheating and match fixing, and have activated systems and processes to monitor, detect, and sanction players and teams for cheating and corruption. While a step in the right direction, unfortunately these policies are inconsistent across Leagues and games, only applying to players participating and are inconsistently sanctioned, often without recourse, in contrast to more robust rights of appeal in traditional sports governance systems.

Governance models

The integrity and safeguarding concerns witnessed in esports poses the question of how esports can ameliorate these challenges through a governance structure that is both sustainable and universally accepted, whilst remaining relevant to the unique features of the esports landscape. To understand the governance options most suitable for esports, it is first important to identify the key stakeholders of the esports ecosystem and the current esports governance frameworks, in addition to the barriers and enablers to effective governance.

Currently the fragmented nature of governance in the sector is not optimal. However, recent moves towards a network administration model, addressing the interdependence of multiple stakeholders, is promising (Peng et al., 2020). While traditional fragmented governance across the ecosystem has stemmed from the commercially driven focus and publisher market power, the increased partnerships with sponsors, governments, media, and sports accompanying growth of esports have placed pressure upon esports to demonstrate reputational risk mitigation through robust governance. The COVID-19-induced investment in esports by traditional sports to diversify revenues and enhance relevance with next generation consumers are also motivations for esports to align governance practices and social responsibility to positively impact their communities and participants. While governance models from sport are of interest, esports needs to integrate a model that aligns with its unique audiences, ownership structures, digital nature, and global landscape. Governance will need to be flexible and simple to accommodate multiple cultures and jurisdictions, and a rapidly evolving gaming landscape.

A brief overview of governance options emerging in esports, whether replicating those structures in sports, self-regulatory, or hybrid systems follows. Recent esports governance case studies are also featured in the case box. While the current state of esports governance is evolving, the ultimate model will reflect a highly networked, adaptable, and integrated model with both national and world sports governance. Any governance and policy framework will need to engage esports at both the apex and foundational levels, including private owners and participants, both recreational and professional. Prior research on policy development specifically affecting youth and young stakeholders suggests a need to engage young people as rights bearers (Arunkumar et al., 2019), and a mutual understanding of youth as agents in the policy process. Stakeholder theory, well adopted in corporate governance, supports this approach in consulting and accounting for all interests impacted by actions of the industry (Jones et al., 2018; Westberg et al., 2017) and developing an inclusive policy process in the complex esports ecosystem. This approach would have a particular advantage in the esports context, by benefiting not only commercial interests dominating the sector, but also vulnerable participants and broader society. Indeed, the potential for esports to facilitate social outcomes is strong, with many examples from education to sustainability already emerging globally, these will be discussed in detail in a future chapter (Chapter 3). At a practical level, public and private stakeholders can play an important role in monitoring, evaluating, and ensuring compliance by governance bodies and the publishers. Even though most governance frameworks are non-mandatory, compliance with such best practices can enhance the legitimacy of esports governance organisations, publishers' codes, and esports generally.

While consensus in governance exists in traditional sports at global and national levels through a plethora of federations and governing bodies, there is no dominant governance entity relating to esports, which continues to be primarily self-regulated. The main governance legitimacy is with the game publishers (e.g., Riot games), each with idiosyncratic governing approaches. For example, Riot introduced The Valorant Global Competition Policy, applying to Valorant competitions and covering everything from competitor age to approved team names and acceptable uniforms. Players are forbidden from cheating, match-fixing, gambling, and accepting gifts, playing under another person's Riot ID, or using any unapproved devices in a tournament's match area. This rule also forbids players from accessing social media while in a match area and use of any abusive or offensive language while participating in a Valorant event (Riot Games, 2020). While these types of policies are a positive example of the current self-regulatory landscape, they are only applicable to one competition and its participants and have limited powers of enforcement.

This lack of integration of best practice standards effectively fragments esports governance across the ecosystem, resulting in significant compliance limitations, despite good intentions brought with self-regulation (Geeraert, 2019). However, several independent esports governance bodies have been established. For example, the World Esports Association (WESA) established by ESL is the first pro-gamer union and has adopted the WADA banned substance list. A key governance initiative by the eight esports commercial organisations forming WESA includes the creation of an arbitration court as an unbiased legal framework for resolving legal issues and disputes including contract disputes, prize money claims, and player representation. WESA is a first-of-its kind organisation geared towards standardising competitive video-gaming (Tribbey, 2016).

The Esports Integrity Commission (ESIC) (previously known as Esports Integrity Coalition) has also been established to eliminate match fixing, corruption, and other integrity issues (Keiper et al., 2017). The ESIC has been one of the most successful governance attempts within the esports industry and the fundamental characteristics of ESIC and how they are trying to support the integrity and regulatory needs of the international esports sector is outlined the next case study.

Another global entity, the International Esports Federation (IESF), comprising of 107 national member signatories, leads global standards in relation to certification, competitions, and player management, and, as a signatory, is also WADA compliant (IESF, 2021). Examples of governance mechanisms introduced by IESF include an anti-doping policy and a gender equality policy, but jurisdiction only extends to international competitions among signatory nations (IESF, 2021). There are also several national esports federations, positioning mostly as esports industry advocates rather than as governing bodies. For example, the Korean Esports Association is a federation integrated into the South Korean Ministry for Culture, Sport, and Tourism with power to regulate the esports sector from players to businesses. The Australian Esports Association (AESA, 2021) aims to elevate

Case Study: The Esports Integrity Commission

ESL founded the Esports Integrity Commission (ESIC) in 2015, to establish a widely accepted integrity plan accepted across the esports industry. ESIC recruited industry stakeholders and created a programme of rules, regulations, and codes as an overarching integrity function code for esports. ESIC takes responsibility for prevention and investigation and prosecution of all forms of cheating. Currently esports lacks regulation and governance and there are no coherent, credible bodies to work with around an integrity code. ESIC has begun the process of creating a unified set of regulations to deal with corruption in esports. *ESIC* programme consists of five key elements:

1. Principles
2. Code of Ethics
3. Code of Conduct to govern behaviour of participants
4. Anti-Corruption Code, a code to deal with offences
5. Anti-Doping Code

The Integrity Commissioner will help new ESIC members implement the programme.

esports to recognition as a sport to build the sector's credibility, accreditation, and reputation, and therefore, under the governance of relevant legislation and codes pertaining to sport, including anti-discrimination policy. The AESA supports the high-performance level of Australian esports athletes and community participation in esports at all skill levels, cultivating social and elite pathways for athletes, coaches, officials, and administrators.

In this state of consolidation for esports governance, universal governance principles of legitimacy, consistency, transparency, accountability, and enforceability provide firm foundations through which to examine governance issues both peculiar to esports and across all sport, to build consensus around best practice. The establishment of a single international federation, mirroring traditional sports, would provide esports with a united advocacy in diplomacy, and access to funding that may otherwise not be available with fragmented governance mechanisms. Whatever the regulatory framework that esports ultimately embraces, sector support will be contingent upon preserving the commerciality of the sector and control will need to be vested through multiple stakeholder involvement. With global sports federation models being scrutinised for integrity, there is opportunity for esports to introduce a contemporary governance structure to align with the new landscape concerned with both shareholder return and social responsibility in a rapidly evolving technology-based competitive space.

Conclusion

Esports are largely self-regulated, with various national and international governing or advocacy bodies existing alongside the sector. While governance remains fragmented, integrity issues continue to thrive in an absence of both legitimate and universally accepted compliance incentives and consistent oversight. However, the industry has significant opportunity to unite to develop a new model of governance which is sufficiently flexible to balance commercial motives and a rapidly evolving technological landscape, and build legitimacy among global and complex stakeholders, including vulnerable young participants. The power of esports as a universal platform resonating with next generation consumers and as a driver of positive social change can be fully realised if robust governance accompanies its growth.

References

AESA. (2021). *We are the Australian esports association.* ASEA. aesa.org.au/about/
Arunkumar, K., et al. (2019). Conceptualizing youth participation in children's health research: Insights from a youth-driven process for developing a youth advisory council. *Children, 6,* 3. http://doi.org/10.3390/children6010003

Brickell, A. (2017). Addressing integrity and regulatory risks in esports: The responsibility of the whole esports community. *Gaming Law Review*, *20*(8). https://doi.org/10.1089/glr2.2017.21810

Browne, B. (2020, February). Gambling on games: How video games expose children to gambling. In *The Australia institute: Centre for responsible technology*, 1–33. Centre for Responsible Technology. https://australiainstitute.org.au/wp-content/uploads/2020/12/P860-Risks-to-kids-from-video-games-Web.pdf

Chao, L. L. (2017). "You must construct additional pylons": Building a better framework for esports governance. *Fordham Law Review*, *86*(2), 737–765.

Conroy, E., Kowal, M., Toth, A., & Campbell, M. (2021). Boosing: Rank and skill deception in esports. *Entertainment Computing*, *36*, 1–8. https://doi.org/10.1016/j.entcom.2020.100393

Czegledy, P. K. (2021). Esports integrity policies. *Gaming Law Review*, *25*(4), 161–170. https://doi.org/10.1089/glr2.2020.0017

Darvin, L., Vooris, R., & Mahoney, T. (2020). The playing experiences of eSport participants: An analysis of treatment discrimination and hostility in eSport environments. *Journal of Athlete Development and Experience*, *2*(1), 3. https://doi-org.ezproxy.library.uq.edu.au/10.25035/jade.02.01.03

Davey, C., & Lundy, L. (2011). Towards greater recognition of the right to play: An analysis of article 31 of the UNCRC. *Children & Society*, *25*(1), 3–14. https://doi.org/10.1111/j.1099-0860.2009.00256.x

Drummond, A., & Sauer, J. (2018). Video game loot boxes are psychologically akin to gambling. *Natural Human Behavior*, *2*, 530–532. http://doi.org/10.1038/s41562-018-0360-1

Funk, D., Pizzo, A., & Baker, B. (2018). Esport management: Embracing eSport education and research opportunities. *Sport Management Review*, *21*(1), 7–13. https://doi.org/10.1016/j.smr.2017.07.008

Geeraert, A. (2019). The limits and opportunities of self-regulation: Achieving international sport federations' compliance with good governance standards. *European Sport Management Quarterly*, *19*(4), 520–538. https://doi.org/10.1080/16184742.2018.1549577

Ghoshal, A. (2019). Ethics in esports. *Gaming in Law Review*, *23*(5), 338–343. http://doi.org/10.1089/glr2.2019.2357

Goslin, A. (2017, April 13). Tainted minds scandal: What we know and what's disputed. *Rift Herald*. www.riftherald.com/2017/3/30/15042300/tainted-minds-scandal-oce-lol-opl

Graham, A. (2015, July 24). Anti-doping in esports: World's largest gaming organization will test for PEDs. *The Guardian News*. www.theguardian.com/technology/2015/jul/23/anti-doping-in-e-sports-worlds-largest-gaming-organization-will-test-for-peds

Hayward, A. (2019, January 2). The 10 highest-earning esports organizations of 2018 by total winnings. *The Esports Observer*. https://esportsobserver.com/10-earning-esports-orgs -2018/

Hallmann, K., & Giel, T. (2018). eSports – Competitive sports or recreational activity? *Sport Management Review*, *21*(1), 14–20. https://doi.org/10.1016/j.smr.2017.07.011

Holden, J., & Baker III, T. (2019). The econtractor? Defining the esports employment relationship. *American Business Law Journal, 56*(2), 391–440. https://doi.org/10.1111/ablj.12141

Hollist, K. (2015). Time to be grown-ups about video gaming: The rising esports industry and the need for regulation. *Arizona Law Review, 57*, 823–847.

IESF. (2021). *About IESF*. World Esports IESF. https://iesf.org/about

Intergalactic Gaming. (2019, April 29). The impact of disproportionate power and immaturity in the esports industry. *Intergalactic Gaming*. https://intergalacticgaming.medium.com/the-impact-of-disproportionate-power-and-immaturity-in-the-esports-industry-bdd487358356

Jang, W. W., Byon, K. K., Baker III, T. A., & Tsuji, Y. (2020). Mediating effect of esports content live streaming in the relationship between esports recreational gameplay and esports event broadcast. *Sport, Business and Management: An International Journal. 11*(1), 89–108. https://doi.org/10.1108/SBM-10-2019-0087

Johri, A. (2020). Cashing in on the esports phenomenon: Increasing awareness on ethical issues and governance challenges. *Journal for Sports Law Policy & Governance, 2*, 41.

Jones, T. M., Harrison, J. S., & Felps, W. (2018). How applying instrumental stakeholder theory can provide sustainable competitive advantage. *Academy of Management Review, 43*(3), 371–391. https://doi.org/10.5465/amr.2016.0111

Keiper, M., Manning, R., Jenny, S., Olrich, T., & Croft, C. (2017). Reason to LoL at LoL: The addition of esports to intercollegiate athletic departments. *Journal for the Study of Sports and Athletes in Education, 11*, 143–160. doi:10.1080/19357397.2017.1316001

Kelly, S. J., Derrington, S., & Star, S. (2021). Governance challenges in esports: A best practice framework for addressing integrity and wellbeing issues. *International Journal of Sport Policy and Politics*, 1–18.

King, D., & Delfabbro, P. (2019). Video game monetization (e.g., 'loot boxes'): A blueprint for practical social responsibility measures. *International Journal of Mental Health and Addiction, 17*, 166–179. http://doi.org/10.1007/s11469-018-0009-3

Kozelco, D. (2021, June 18). Fighting fraud and match fixing in esports-ESIC refer team AKUMA case to valve. *LawInSport*. www.lawinsport.com/topics/item/fighting-fraud-and-match-fixing-in-esports-esic-refer-team-akuma-case-to-valve

Li, W., Mills, D., & Nower, L. (2019). The relationship of loot box purchases to problem video gaming and problem gambling. *Addictive Behaviors, 97*, 27–34. https://doi.org/10.1016/j.addbeh.2019.05.016

Macey, J., Abarbanel, B., & Hamari, J. (2020). What predicts esports betting? A study on consumption of video games, esports, gambling and demographic factors. *New Media & Society, 23*(6), 148–1505. https://doi.org/10.1177/1461444820908510

Mitchell, F. (2014, March 13). 'League of legends' pro attempts suicide after match-fixing scandal. *Dotesports*. https://dotesports.com/league-of-legends/news/league-of-legends-promise-suicide-match-fixing-160

Peng, Q., Dickson, G., Scelles, N., Grix, J., & Brannagan, P. M. (2020). Esports governance: Exploring stakeholder dynamics. *Sustainability, 12*(19), 8270. https://doi.org/10.3390/su12198270

Riot Games. (2020, October 16). Competitive policies & rules for Valorant esports. *Riot Games*. https://playvalorant.com/en-us/news/esports/competitive-policies-rules-for-valorant-esports/

Scholz, T. M. (2019). Unwritten governing principles. In *eSports is business* (pp. 101–116). Palgrave Pivot.

Sporttechie. (2020, May 8). Activision Blizzard partners with sportradar to safeguard esports betting. *SportTechie*. www.sporttechie.com/activision-blizzard-esports-sportradar-betting/

Stubbs, M. (2020, May 15). 'Dota 2' team newbee banned from Chinese competitions for match fixing. *Forbes*. www.forbes.com/sites/mikestubbs/2020/05/15/dota-2-team-newbee-banned-from-chinese-competitions-for-match-fixing/?sh=1d0bc49d4dbe

Tribbey, C. (2016, May 23). Broadcasters take long view with esports. *Broadcasting & Cable*, New York, N.Y., *146*(20), 24–25.

Westberg, K., Stavros, C., Smith, A. C. T., Newton, J., Lindsay, S., Kelly, S. J., Beus, S., & Adair, D. (2017). Exploring the wicked problem of athlete and consumer vulnerability in sport. *Journal of Social Marketing*, *7*(1), 94–112. https://doi.org/10.1108/JSOCM-07-2016-0035

Windholz, E. (2020). Governing esports: Public policy, regulation, and the law. *Sports Law Ejournal*. https://doi.org/10.53300/001c.13241

Wolf, J. (2016, May 9). Riot games kicks renegades, team impulse, team dragon knights from NA LCS and NACS. *ESPN*. www.espn.com/esports/story/_/id/15494634/riot-games-kicks-renegades-team-impulse-team-dragon-knights-na-lcs-nacs

Wong, J. (2020). More than just a game: The labor and employment issues within eSports. *UNLV Gaming Law Journal*, *11*(1), 123–152.

Xiao, L., & Henderson, L. (2019). Towards an ethical game design solution to loot boxes: A commentary on king and delfabbro. *International Journal of Mental Health and Addiction*, *19*, 177–192. https://doi.org/10.1007/s11469-019-00164-4

3 Esports as a mechanism for social change

Key Questions

1. *What is esports' relationship with social change?*
2. *How does esports connect with educational, economic, and social agendas?*
3. *How can esports be better utilised for its social change properties?*

Introduction

The shared interest and passion held by gamers who inhabit and reside in esports environments brings individuals together and offers a sense of belonging, community, and support. Research has highlighted that esports communities encourage and produce strong social opportunities for interaction, bonding, and building social capital (Martončik, 2015; Trepte et al., 2012). This leads to the formation of friendships and can support both personal and social development. Its potential has been realised within educational contexts, as educators are seeing academic and social benefits, especially for disengaged students who may typically not be inspired or influenced by traditional sports (Hennick, 2020). Kids in the Game, a US-based Sport for Development organisation uses esports programming to compliment physical activity in New York middle schools, to aid the development of transferable skills (Samples, 2019). Esports social properties and role as a mechanism for positive change will be explored in multiple ways to highlight the evolving understanding of esports social impacts.

In this chapter key themes of social change are introduced in relation to esports participation as well as targeted interventions via esports as part of social change agendas. The core themes include, esports communities, esports employability and careers, esports and social good, and esports and Sport for Development (SfD). These themes will be, partly, explored through data collected in a 2019 by two of the authors of this book. The

DOI: 10.4324/9781003213598-3

'CSR & Social Opportunities within esports' research project[1] will provide diverse expert perspectives and voices within this chapter. In particular significant statements made by esports players and stakeholders are presented to highlight the opportunities and challenges of utilising esports as a social change tool. For clarity, esports players included those competing on a regular basis within a formally established team or university setting and stakeholder groups included esports' national governing bodies, trade unions, game publishers, teams and gamers, tournament organisers, media entities, as well as Sport for Development (SfD) organisations who planned to or were using esports interventions as part of their strategy. Case studies will also be presented to contextualise esports activities and social outcomes.

Esports communities – how can you be a community if you don't see each other?

"Esport is centred on the community" Interviewee 1- Esports Stakeholder
One of the common misconceptions of esports is the assumed isolated nature of participating. Yet, social interconnectivity, shared values, and behaviours cultivated through esports participation create a sense of community amongst players. Beyond the common usage of the term community as a physically bounded entity, there exists a growing cohort of esports participants who share interests, passions, and a common (self-perceived) community identity. As participants in the aforementioned research explained, "it's a community culture with unique fandom surrounding it. Each game/ title has a unique community" (Focus group 3 – USA). Going beyond individual identities and experiences of participation, community thinking in virtual environments revolved around the idea of esports as a space of cultural assimilation and community building.

Research suggests that the idea of community is central and highly important to esports players across all levels of competition (Hayday et al., 2021). When speaking with gamers they often described their esports experiences in relation to *the* community as they described the social norms of *their* people. Esports players are joined by their common interest and desire to play online, connect to other players who share their game and format preferences and belong to a wider community of gamers and enthusiasts. As one gamer explained, "I think esports are a great way to bring like-minded people together", (Focus group 3 – USA). The central component of community is seemingly very important to individuals involved with esports, and it is the notion of community that continues to drive esports connection to social change on a personal and interpersonal level. As one esports player explained, "We are not isolated, we are a proper community, regardless of outside perceptions" (Focus group 3 – USA).

Another assumption surrounding esports communities is the insular nature of its participation, however, one participant articulated that esports communities also include those who spectate. "There's absolutely a community aspect to esports that's incredibly important, because if there wasn't a community or a fan-base around esports there wouldn't be audiences watching those games" (Interviewee 1). In this regard, esports becomes more than a cultural phenomenon but a legitimate tool for developing and enhancing social identity and building social capital inside and outside of virtual spaces (Cunningham et al., 2018). The notion of inclusivity is central to this discourse, with the assumption that virtual participation removes traditional discrimination associated with race, gender, and physical ability. However, this is highly contested by scholars who have described highly fractious communities and online toxicity in the form of racism, sexism, and abuse against the LGBTQ communities (Hayday et al., 2021; Madden et al., 2021; Shaw, 2012). In this case, esports is not that distinct nor free from the negative trends seen in mainstream sport including racism seen across international football or sexism seen within sport marketing and media (Fink, 2019).

Although esports is designed for competitive play in virtual spaces, esports communities have emerged in physical spaces as well. The formation of esports hubs, cafes, and gaming centres have added a physical dimension to community building and social cohesion for esports participants and spectators. The in-person esports experience goes beyond esports cafes and gaming hubs, and now intersects with global sports events like the Olympics, university, and college sport clubs (there are currently 175 US colleges that offer varsity esports programmes recognised by the National Association of Collegiate esports) and non-sport public events (Esports.net, 2019). Large-scale esports competitions have seen the virtual and the physical boundaries diminish, with the growth of live in-person tournaments and events. Whilst this is often viewed as a result of the commercialisation, professionalisation, and event marketing in the esports sector, it has created new opportunities for social engagement and interaction. Esports communities, and its social impacts, are no longer bounded by virtual spaces, creating new opportunities for social change agendas to be developed in both physical and virtual formats.

Esports for social good?

Not to be confused with formal development for social change agendas, as adopted by highly institutionalised actors, for example the United Nations (UN), esports for social good is defined by local actors and groups who use esports to promote and support local populations. This may include using esports to promote health messages and healthy lifestyles, 'levelling up' (a term used to describe enhancing equality and equal opportunities) and providing inclusive opportunities or outreach work in the community. Esports for social good often aligns to Corporate Social Responsibility (CSR) agendas or partnerships with local charities. For example, the charity Gamers Outreach as part of the ESL initiative for 'Gaming for Good' provides children in hospitals access to video games. Gamers Outreach was founded by a group of high school gamers in Michigan, US, while volunteering at local hospitals. ESL helped to raise awareness and donated proceeds to support Gamers Outreach and their network of nearly 200 hospitals and more than 1.25 million children (ESL Gaming GmbH, 2021).

Another example of esports' ability to support social good is presented in the next case study, through esports team LDN UTD.

Case Study: LDN UTD

Written by Oliver Weingarten – CEO and Founder of LDN UTD

"LDN UTD is an organisation based in London, England, that uses gaming and esports to promote healthy lifestyles and address social issues. We have three verticals relating to: the development of gamers and the pathway from grassroots to professional, content creators, and host physical and online events to raise awareness of today's social issues. We partner with universities, traditional sports organisations, local Government, and talent to deliver our strategy. Our motto is Esports for Good. We are "For Gamers that give a ****", why do we have this? To ensure people know what we stand for, that we care about the issues they do, and to try and make us memorable.

Because there are issues all over the world that need to be addressed, and what better medium is there, than the fastest growing consumer industry of esports to raise awareness and try and make an impact. There are over two billion gamers in the world. Accelerated by the COVID-19 pandemic, technology has seen exponential growth in the sector, and we know Gen Z care about social issues. When we have an issue, we believe should be addressed, we look to see how it can authentically be delivered, and the best mechanism to raise awareness with our community. We work with partners linked to three priority areas:

1. **Mayor of London (education and transferable skills)** – We targeted Boroughs of London and worked with outreach partners to deliver two weeks of workshops partnering with academics and sports org and esports partners. Workshops included social media management, public speaking, video editing, and production. All skill sets for working in esports that can be transferred to other industries. Excitingly: students at Conisborough College attended each workshop as part of their school curriculum!

2. **Rio Ferdinand Foundation (diversity and equality)** – First esports event that the Foundation has used to showcase its messaging and raise awareness of the Foundation itself. Whilst there was a FIFA tournament which included celebrity participation, the powerful messaging was delivered through interviews with South African PDC darts player Devon Peterson, BAFTA winning actor Colin Salmon, and others including M-People's Heather Small alongside LDN UTD creator Lauren who compared their challenges as technology has developed.

3. **P Money (#GrimeAgainstKnives)** – An opportunity to get youths off the streets for an evening of gaming. LDN UTD worked with the local authority and police, alongside local resident P-Money, the grime artist, hence the title #GrimeAgainstKnives. This was a one-night live event.

We bring in relevant talent and influencers to promote the campaigns and host physical or online events which contain esports content interspersed with the education content. This is a novel way of addressing social issues. The eyeballs to the Twitch stream show there is substantial interest in the campaigns we address".

Esports social good initiatives span a range of contexts and issues from raising awareness and resilience on local crime trends, health and wellbeing, diversity and equality, and skill-based levelling up strategies. Local initiatives like the aforementioned examples through the work of LDN UTD and partnering organisations (local authority departments and esports publishers) are creating credible opportunities for the esports sector to contribute to community development and support charity organisations.

Tackling social issues for social change via esports

Beyond bringing people together, both virtually and increasingly in person, esports' capacity to support change is being recognised and explored by charities, esports stakeholders and the wider gaming community. This is being achieved in several ways, firstly through adaptive technologies, secondly utilising communication opportunities within esports, and thirdly strengthening partnerships with social change movements and actors. In this section we highlight the evolving role of esports to tackle social issues in the context of disability, climate change, and gender.

The relative anonymity of virtual participation assumes a level of protection from discrimination in esports, and whilst this has been contested and toxicity remains a contemporary issue, esports' rapid uptake has accelerated its adoption by previous sceptics and those who recognise its potential to offer something new to their social change agendas. Empowering people with disabilities and providing inclusive spaces for people with disabilities is one area that has seen esports' ability to break social boundaries. For example, the charity AbleGamers has seen people with disabilities participate freely in esports and influence the sector through the training of over 200 developers to make accessible games (The AbleGamers Foundation Inc, 2021).

Case Study: AbleGamers

People with disabilities are at a heightened risk of social isolation. However, AbleGamers knows that video games can be the perfect gateway to community participation, lifelong friendships, and unforgettable shared experiences. That's why it's crucial to ensure these experiences are developed with accessibility as a priority and inclusion as the goal. For over a decade and a half, AbleGamers has been pushing the inclusive efforts of the industry forward by training and consulting studios while connecting them directly with players who can share their personal experiences.

AbleGamers has created the largest impanelled group of people with disabilities in the world. The Player Panel programme is a collection of hundreds of players with disabilities who advise the gaming industry. AbleGamers are dedicated to increasing representation and understanding of people with disabilities is evident throughout their work. They have empowered thousands of people to connect with the gaming world and have created multiple adaptive hardware solutions by working with engineering teams and research partners. So far, AbleGamers have helped 3,568 people with disabilities through Peer Counselling and assistance with hardware and software challenges. They have:

1) Engineered 49 custom equipment solutions for people with disabilities through the work of their in-house engineering team.
2) Trained almost 200 developers to make accessible games.
3) Connected 328 players with disabilities to the industry since 2018, empowering them to lend their voice to create a more accessible gaming world.

(The AbleGamers Foundation Inc, 2021).

The example of AbleGamers demonstrates the opportunities esports provide for engaging and including marginal groups and individuals most vulnerable to enhance social exclusion.

Esports and climate change

Climate change and environmental sustainability have become both a global crisis and priority. As a sector associated with innovation and transnational connectivity, esports stakeholders recognise their responsibility to commit to a low carbon future and tackle climate change. In 2021, The Global Esports Federation (GEF) joined and committed to the 'Sports for Climate Action' initiative by the United Nations Framework Convention on Climate Change (UNFCCC). Paul J. Foster, CEO of Global Esports Federation, claimed "Esports and gaming are powerful platforms for connection, for creating awareness and to generate impact in combating climate change, across all parts of the diverse ecosystem" (Esports Insider, 2021). This newly formed alliance between the esports sector and the climate change agenda reinforces esports' role and ability to contribute to social change on a global stage.

The 2021 commitment was not the first esports-climate change partnership. In 2019, the United Nations (UN) Environment Program in collaboration with video gaming stakeholders launched the 'Playing for the Planet Alliance'. This was formalised during the UN's Climate Summit in the same year, and saw companies commit to reducing their emissions via a range of initiatives to support the global environmental agenda. Strategies including reducing plastic consumption and use, planting trees, and integrating green activations in games were introduced (Playing for The Planet Alliance, 2021). Esports have been recognised as cultural phenonema that can be used to influence and mobilise climate change awareness and behaviours. Esports playing platforms have been positioned to share information and reinforce key messages on climate change and environmental critical issues. Such collaborations between esports and climate change organisations provide innovative and potentially powerful ways to raise awareness of climate issues at a global scale which are very attractive to global organisations such as the United Nations. In practice, esports have been able to be creative with their climate change initiatives. For example, Minecraft asked its users to create their own coral reefs, and in just two days, players placed ten million coral blocks, which triggered Minecraft to donate to The Nature Conservatory to aid coral reef conversation (Smith, 2020). This highlights esports significant ability to create traction for climate change and conservation movements, by mobilising its esports users base.

Esports and gender

The experiences of women and girls in gaming and esports environments have been a contentious area for the sector. Whilst gender neutrality is assumed as a special feature of esports participation, research suggests that women and girls are exposed to harmful behaviours, a lack of representation and toxic cultures (Hayday & Collison, 2021). In a recent piece of research conducted by Darvin et al. (2021), it is suggested that a 'glass monitor' exists in esports that inhibits career access and advancement within the sport. Despite some traction within the sector to tackle gender discrimination, elite-level women esports employees encounter numerous barriers and obstacles (Darvin et al., 2021), the industry maintains a hostile culture for women and girls plagued by harassment and participants experience toxic masculinity (Rogstad, 2021). In a 2021 review of research literature on gender and esports, three core themes were identified. Firstly, issues of the construction of masculinity are not immune in esports, secondly, online harassment is significant, and thirdly, gendered expectations are no different within esports spaces to mainstream sports (Rogstad, 2021). The review concluded that although esports and traditional sports are clearly different, issues of masculinity, athleticism, and competition fuel gender inequalities in the same manner. Despite, increasing participation of women and girls, more action and knowledge is needed on how hyper masculine cultures can be countered and how gender positive cultures can be cultivated within esports platforms and organisational settings.

A non-profit organisation based in Sweden called 'Female Legends' has responded to gender challenges within esports by creating a very clear mandate and offering a number of strategic programmes, strategies, and support mechanisms to encourage safe and inclusive participation (Female Legends, 2020). On their website they claim:

Case Study: Female Legends

We firmly believe there is no physical difference between the genders when it comes to esports prowess, yet we see a significantly lower rate of participation from women on all levels. A study of 2000 Swedish youth in 2015 shows that girls play just as many video games as boys up until puberty, when girls stop. Notably they could not find more than three female participants in the age span 17–18 claiming to play any esports title. Another study by the Swedish anti-bullying organization Friends uncovered that one in five women had been harassed during the previous year, contrary to one in ten for the men. We also know that women who game are more likely to head into STEM fields, which include game development, where they are otherwise underrepresented. Female Legends will work toward not being needed, and believe we will be so when we see:

1)   A gender-equal and low level of harassment in gaming
2)   A significant share of female participants in esports on all levels
3)   Equal and inclusive workplaces in all areas related to gaming

(Female Legends, 2020).

Despite, the challenges esports are facing, there are significant opportunities to counter and mitigate for gender discrimination and harmful behaviours. Esports are intrinsically gender neutral, due to the reduced physical dimension of competing, therefore, esports participation has the potential to operate in the absence of traditional gender stereotypes and disparity (Kim, 2017). That is not to say that exchanges made on esports platforms are absent from hyper-masculine narratives nor over-sexualised commentaries that create potentially abusive online environments. However, there are burgeoning efforts to boost female participation through initiatives which aim to enhance diversity and female agency to address such challenges within the industry (Associated Press, 2019; BBC, 2016; Women in Games, 2021). Through strategies such as Women in Esports we have also seen the creation of female only Valorant tournaments called 'The Huntress Trials' (Nicholson, 2021). Some may question if this approach is heightening gender separation, yet it could also be seen as a first step in encouraging females to compete at an elite level, increasing exposure and the creation of role models. In this regard we might position esports as having the potential to support inclusive practices, but the challenges lie in its operational mechanisms and the social lens in which to focus gender specific social change agendas.

Esports' desires to connect to global sport and non-sport agendas could also create another opportunity for women's empowerment and representation. The United Nations Sustainable Development Goals (SDGs) highlight the process of human development in relation to social inclusion and gender equality. SDG 5 aims to achieve gender equality and empower all women and girls, and creates a framework for esports entities to align in order to focus their attention, policies, and efforts to achieve gender inclusivity. The potential alignment between the esports sector and the SDGs is already being formalised. For example, The Global Esports Federation and the United Nations Educational, Scientific and Cultural Organization (UNESCO) have publicly announced their intention to collaborate and contribute towards the achievement of the SDGs. Each organisation will bring specific expertise and focus to facilitate the progress of four SDGs, aimed at empowering the youth of the world, in particular; SDG 3: good health and wellbeing, SDG 4: quality education, SDG 5: gender equality, and SDG 17: partnerships for the goals (Global Esports Federation, 2021). This partnership demonstrates a clear intention from the esports sector to strengthen its social agenda, and in particular contribute to gender equality progress and reform.

Research suggests that if esports are to be taken seriously, and indeed implemented meaningfully within social change agendas the sector must align with movements and global agendas outside of itself. The practice of esports may have social benefits and outcomes but conceptual modelling and theoretical alignment strengthen the approach to deliver esports and gaming for specific impacts. One potential opportunity for esports in the context of social change lies in the established Sport for Development sector.

Sport for development through esports

Sport has featured heavily in international social development agendas for over 20 years. The SfD movement has been a policy, advocacy, and engagement space that has created an increasingly institutionalised and professionalised home for sport within the broader development context (Collison et al., 2018). The connections made between sport and development are centred on the assumptions that sport can bring, often young, people together to socially interact in a shared interest. Sport is positioned as a mechanism that provides opportunities to deliver and reinforce positive messages and information, and develops important soft, emotional, and life skills i.e., communication, teamwork, leadership, resiliency, informal education, conflict resolution, and reflection. Social change is a sub-field of SfD that positions sport as a catalyst to build social capacity, develop social relationships and awareness, and create community cohesion (Sherry et al., 2015). This is a multifaceted endeavour and development field that provides a wide canvas or contour for intervention focusing on goals and delivery methods. Social change is not bound by social outcomes but an intersecting element of wider development impacts. Participants in SfD programmes focused on empowerment and enhancing social identity, capital, and capacity leveraged from their user group position to volunteer and coaching roles, strengthens the social and economic mobility outcomes of sport interventions (Peachey et al., 2015).

For example, a project called 'Waves for Change: Surf Therapy' based in the townships on the outskirts of Cape Town, South Africa, is an organisation that seeks to transform the lives of young people exposed to violence and trauma. The SfD methodology in this case is weekly after-school surfing activities, and in-group and individual therapy sessions. The programme works with young people to deal with their experiences, increase their emotional resilience and confidence, and gain new skills and qualifications so they are better equipped to make positive choices and feel more optimistic about their future (Wave for Change, 2021).

The types of sport endorsed by the SfD sector and implementing partners are often classified as mainstream sports and physical activity, most often team games such as football, cricket, basketball, rugby, and netball. Such sports attract transnational partnership opportunities, connect to global networks, and appeal to significant numbers of participants. Mainstream sport acts as a hook to draw in communities and participants in order to facilitate opportunities for engagement and deliver targeted development activities. Yet is this established approach to SfD through traditional sports still relevant given the changing and digitalised nature of today's world? Whilst there have been numerous debates surrounding the evidence base for SfD impact, in its traditional design, important questions must be posed in order to account for SfD's resistance to new sporting trends and accessing populations not drawn to traditional sports activities. Another limitation of SfD is the lack of transnational connections created for user groups. In its current format, SfD projects are mostly implemented in isolation from other interventions and have limited opportunities for participants to engage with others outside of their communities. Yet, esports offers a virtual environment which can enhance SfD programming and heightens the prospect of long-term connectivity through digital mechanisms.

Recognising the development potential and limitations of mainstream sport and the need to access a wider critical mass of young people for development and educational outcomes, a new agenda may be necessary for the sustainability of the SfD sector and local social change initiatives (Loat, 2021). Esports to this point, sits outside of the mainstream thinking of SfD stakeholders and civil society movements and this is widening the gap between those who participate within development programmes and those who do not. Despite its global popularity and exponential growth and appeal to youth populations, esports is seemingly misunderstood as a potential development strategy. This has significant impacts for actors working towards the achievement of the SDGs, national development agendas, community empowerment and capacity building agendas. Esports is an underutilised mechanism that could contribute to SfD and civil society programme offerings as part of a holistic approach to social change. Social inclusion is one SfD driver that could be supported through esports programming, as its very nature has inclusive properties. Esports' popularity cannot be ignored, therefore esports could be the hook for the next generation of youth not drawn to football pitches or mainstream physical activities. Experts in the SfD field have been enhanced their interest in the potential sub-field of Esports for Development (eSfD) as an additional facet of a holistic approach to sports offerings in development settings. The next case study highlights recent conceptualisations of eSfD.

Sport for Development – Expert Case Study: Richard Loat – SfD practitioner

In 2004, W. Chan Kim and Renée Mauborgne redefined the world by dividing it into red oceans or blue oceans. Red oceans are all existing industries today where industry boundaries, stakeholders, and audiences are defined through competition, and one only succeeds by outperforming their rivals. Their analogy assumed that zero-sum competition is so cutthroat it turns the ocean a bloody red.

Beyond the red oceans lie blue oceans which are market spaces that are undefined or definable and where industry players, by differentiating themselves, create new demand. Blue ocean strategies end up creating and capturing uncontested market space where competition doesn't exist. In blue oceans the market boundaries, stakeholders, and industry structures are malleable and are shaped in real time by the actions and values of existing stakeholders.

The sports industry has seen its share of blue oceans over the last few decades. Mainstream cricket was disrupted by blue-ocean domestic T20 leagues, the most successful being the Indian Premier League. Rather than competing for audiences that are drawn to the longer formats of the game, a new format cultivated new audiences, commercial interests, and societal benefits. FIBA, the global governing body of basketball, set sail to oceans blue by investing in a new half-court, 3-on-3 format for its universality, young, urban, and positive image, and its accessibility due to the limited infrastructure and equipment required to play. The Ultimate Fighting Championship (UFC) and Formula E are also both examples of blue oceans created within their respective sports, combat sports and motorsports.

Nurturing blue ocean strategy cultivates innovation and broadens spheres of influence. Historically, blue oceans have enabled the evolution of industries whilst also unlocking cost savings and modes of increased sustainability. The advent of competitive video games is the newest blue ocean in the sports industry. Esports has catalysed new broadcasting mechanisms, attracted new audiences, and redefined the laws of sporting fandom. This nascent digital medium has also laid the groundwork for a more inclusive playing field while its mobile interoperability is rapidly making it one of the most accessible sports.

SFD methodologies address society's most systemic challenges and SFD can in many ways be considered a blue ocean within the humanitarian development sector. The early years of the SFD blue ocean brought new stakeholders to the development sector, increasing the resources available for a sector that has historically competed for a stagnant amount of aid funding. As an established sector, SFD now finds itself saturated and looking to enable the growth of existing programmes without hindering the emergence of new methodologies. Esports represents a strategic blue ocean not just for the sports industry but for SFD too.

Blue oceans are evolving spaces. The actions and values of stakeholders within the space shape it. Therefore, the nascent field, or ocean, of esports for development (eSfD) is very definable with new methodologies being developed, spheres of influence being introduced, and evidence mounting for the value of esports as a tool for change. Traditional sports have physical and infrastructure limits which limit possible impact. For example, the SFD methodology behind surf therapy, a mental health intervention, isn't possible without a body of water. Similarly, skateboarding methodologies require a skate park or halfpipe, and team based SFD methodologies aren't possible if you cannot congregate. eSfD's digital nature and growing digital connectivity changes the spatial requirements to engage SFD beneficiaries.

If we consider eSfD to be a blue ocean within SFD, we need to acknowledge that we don't know the shape it will take. As a blue ocean strategy within SFD, esports is not a plug-and-play replacement for sports within existing methodologies. It is likely to disrupt the way in which we apply sport within SFD methodologies. Developing a SFD methodology requires the right sport and right social issue based on local context. The contextual agnosticism and digital nature of esports removes one SFD design limitation, subsequently increasing its applicability to thematic issues. Without physical design limitations, eSfD methodologies could very likely address issues that SFD has never been able to address.

Presently, esports for change work is conceptually basic from cause-based fundraising through video games, to grassroots efforts to tackling the esport's inclusivity issues by increasing participation of minority groups. Any SFD methodologies that have incorporated esports have been twinned with physical activity in hybridised models to retain an element of physical activity. There are too few organisations truly looking at an esports-driven theory of change that replaces physical sport entirely within a methodology.

The potential of eSfD is undefinable currently, yet it could introduce new ways of addressing social issues. The esports hook is an opportunity to align eSfD interventions with industry partnerships with as yet unknown impact pathways. The modern spectrum of social issues is also evolving. Climate change, cyber security, automation of the labour force, and urban migration are some of the emerging societal challenges we face and esports is poised to be a central component of future methodologies addressing these issues. Simply put, it is a new platform on which to invent game-changing solutions to emerging global challenges. In the same way that the mp3 digitised the music industry, esports is digitising the sports industry.

Esports is potentially a new evolutionary tool within the sport SfD landscape, recognising its utility to attract new methods of impact that are futureproof. Sustainability remains a key concern for the development sector broadly but sport itself needs to remain relevant to target populations, therefore esports are presented by its advocates as a method that could bring new forms of sustainability to a stagnating sector.

Esports' identity as a tool for social good expands beyond civil society and community engagement. The Sustainable Development Goals (SDGs) for example give a great deal of attention to economic mobility, education opportunities, and investment and investing in young generations. In the next section we consider esports as an educational tool and a platform to enhance digital skills leading to enhanced employment prospects.

Esports, education, and employability

The esports sector has begun to increasingly recognise its obligation and need to engage with education initiatives and invest in employability programmes. In the case of esports, education and employability intersect in very distinct ways. For example, in April 2020, British Esports teamed up with global education publisher Pearson to develop the first esports Business and Technology Education Council (BTEC) qualification. Institutions in the UK and around the world will have the opportunity to offer these new qualifications to students from September 2020, with funding confirmed in the UK from the Education and Skills Funding Agency (British Esports Association, 2021). The newly launched education initiative is driven by the aim

Table 3.1 Esports career pathway

Roles in Esports	Academic Links	Careers in Tech/Digital/STEM Industries
Professional player	Computer science	Cyber security
Coach	ICT	Software development
Shout caster/host	Sciences	Big data and analytics
Analyst	Technology	Cloud solutions
Journalist	Engineering	Network engineering
Observer	Mathematics	Mobile technologies
Admin (Referee)	Creative media	Digital engineering
Broadcast/Production	Business studies	Artificial intelligence
Community/Social media manager	Entrepreneurship	UI-UX design
Team/Player management and operations	Game development	Network management
Streamer/Influencer	Sport	Virtual reality
Video editor/photographer		Software engineering

Source: Adapted from British Esports Association (2021)

of employment within the sector upon certification. This is also highlighted by their esports careers pathway model which has been adapted into a table:

Table 3.1 represents the *thinking* within the esports sector with regards to investment in the future, alignment to essential skills, and strengthening the connection to other industries. The drive to enhance educational partnerships and expanding curriculums within educational settings is gaining traction globally. This is primarily led by those in the technology and innovation space, for example, in a recent article by Hank Chou, Associate Manager, Acer HQ he claims that,

> "As esports gains more popularity among young people, it's a no brainer that schools can adopt this trend to leverage its benefits to facilitate learning and boost students' academic or career performance. . . . As esports start to be considered as high-potential career options, it's imperative to understand the importance of building up a pipeline for self-development (or career development) for student players on campus. By creating an esports-focused community in schools, students can connect their passion with their academic and personal goals."
>
> (Acer Inc, 2021)

The Digital School House (DSH) in the UK provides another example of an organisation which collaborates with Nintendo UK to deliver education through esports. DSH has utilised play-based learning, through organising esports tournaments, to support and advance skill development and knowledge in diverse educational settings. Centred on digital creativity, the overarching aim is to enhance digital skills. DSH's esports tournaments are structured through school, regional, and national competition heats and have so far engaged over 10,000 students. Positive educational outcomes include enhanced soft skills like communication and teamwork, the building of friendships and social bonds, and a heightened interest in technology-based careers (Saeed et al., 2018).

Esports have also been strongly connected to Science, Technology, Engineering, and Mathematics [STEM] learning. During the research project described in the introduction of this chapter, one participant explained, esports is a "new way to attract younger audiences, [build] links to STEM work and can drive female engagement" in those disciplines (Focus Group 1 – UK). The relationship between STEM and esports provides an opportunity to create a pipeline for employment in those sectors, whilst encouraging more diverse and equitable opportunities, in particular for women and minority groups. This trend has been particularly strong in the US, in 2018. For example, the Riot Games director of collegiate esports said that nearly two thirds of their League of Legends players were majoring in STEM fields (Reames, 2018). That is a significant increase from 45% of all undergraduates in 2015 that planned to study STEM subjects (ibid). There-fore, offering and facilitating esports within school settings can increase interest to pursue STEM-related subjects in further education and later in professional contexts.

The opportunities for esports inclusion into educational environments are arguably limitless. Recent research suggests that art and design, and the study of aesthetics should be incorporated into esports education which extends its reach outside of STEM subjects (Lee & Chou, 2021). An esports inclusive curriculum or extra curriculum activities are arguably the gateway into early development and interest in STEM subjects and related fields. The employment sectors associated with esports or other technology, digital, and innovation sectors welcome the provisions and educational initiatives currently operating and have formed partnerships to facilitate educational projects, including Intel, Nintendo, and professional sports clubs. Beyond the realms of esports, young participants are now being encouraged to pur-sue an entrepreneurial mindset when planning for the future, and esports are being recognised for their linkages to broader yet interrelated sectors, such as software development, virtual reality industries, cyber security, digital engineering, and coding. The question may need to be repositioned, why wouldn't schools include esports as part of their curriculums and learning aims?

Conclusion

This chapter has highlighted the importance of community and social bonding to esports participants. It is the social properties and outcomes of playing esports that provides feelings of belonging and kinship. This is sig-nificant to millions of esports users who value being part of transnational and local gaming networks. In recent years esports have seen transforma-tive playing formats in the form of large scale in person tournaments and events, gaming hubs and cafes, and collegiate teams. The in-person formats have challenged the assumption of esports being a pursuit of the socially marginal or isolated. The outward facing accessibility of esports has also led to increased opportunities to promote and advance social change strate-gies and agendas. The social components of esports have been particularly meaningful for marginalised groups, including women and people living with physical impairments. Adaptive technologies, anonymity, and efforts to confront discrimination and online toxicity continue to create entry points for women, marginalised groups, and disabled populations to participate in esports.

Social change, social good, and social development have all been key themes of this chapter. Through key partnerships between esports publishers, the charity sector, the UN, the education sector, and civil society organisations, the social outcomes of esports are beginning to be fully explored and utilised. Esports have arguably brought social innovation and digital entrepreneurship to the Sport for Development (SfD) and social change movements. Esports are also positively disrupting education curriculums and driving STEM related learning in schools, which has already had significant impacts on higher education pathways and the scope of career opportunities leveraged from experience and skills in esports. Arguably, esports are the hook and the mechanism for positive social change and this is only increasing the role of esports in social contexts and global agendas.

The third question posed in this chapter was, How can esports be better utilised for its social change properties? This has proven to be a difficult question to answer based on the progress that has been made thus far. However, the social outcomes and value of esports are is dependent on inclusivity and positive playing experiences. With an enhancement in governance structures and improved cultures tackling online toxicity (see Chapter 4), more women and girls and marginalised groups will be able to benefit from esports communities and educational opportunities. As the social agendas and interventions adopting esports continue to evolve, more partnerships inside and outside of the esports sector will be needed. This is particularly important to maintain esports' use for innovative and intersectional approaches for to social change.

Note

1 This research project was funded by Loughborough University London in 2019. Research was conducted in Loughborough London University, UK and University of California, Berkeley, USA. Participants included esports participants, publishers, stakeholders. Over a period of four months, three workshops (*n*= 65) were hosted, and 14 interviews were conducted.

References

The AbleGamers Foundation Inc. (2021). *The able gamers charity*. Able Gamers. https://ablegamers.org/

Acer Inc. (2021, May 20). Esports: The future of engaging education. *Acer for Education*. https://acerforeducation.acer.com/education-trends/esports-in-education/future-engaging-education/

Associated Press. (2019, January 3). Women in professional esports navigate hyper masculinity and harassment. *Market Watch*. www.marketwatch.com/story/women-in-professional-esports-navigate-hyper-masculinity-and-harassment-2019-01–03

BBC. (2016, November 21). 100 Women 2016: The women challenging sexism in e-sports. *BBC News*. www.bbc.co.uk/news/technology-37992322

British Esports Association. (2021). *Esports and education.* British Esports Association. https://britishesports.org/esports-and-education/

Collison, H., Darnell, S. C., Giulianotti, R., & Howe, P. D. (Eds.). (2018). *Routledge handbook of sport for development and peace.* Routledge.

Cunningham, G. B., Fairley, S., Ferkins, L., Kerwin, S., Lock, D., Shaw, S., & Wicker, P. (2018). eSport: Construct specifications and implications for sport management. *Sport Management Review, 21*(1), 1–6. doi:10.1016/j.smr.2017.11.002

Darvin, L., Holden, J., Wells, J., & Baker, T. (2021). Breaking the glass monitor: Examining the underrepresentation of women in esports environments. *Sport Management Review, 24*(3), 475–499. doi:10.1080/14413523.2021.1891746

ESL Gaming GmbH. (2021). *Gaming for good.* ESL Gaming. https://about.eslgaming.com/portfolio/gaming-for-good/

Esports Insider. (2021, March 22). Global esports federation joins the sports for climate action initiative. *Esports Insider.* www.esportsinsider.com/2021/03/gef-joins-sports-for-climate-action-initiative/

Esports.net. (2019, December 17). US universities continue to develop esports programs. *Esports.net.* www.esports.net/news/industry/us-universities-continue-to-develop-esports-programs/

Female Legends. (2020). *What is female legends?* Female Legends. https://femalelegends.com/english

Fink, J. S. (2019). Sexism in marketing women's sport and female athletes: Ineffective and harmful. In *Routledge handbook of the business of women's sport* (pp. 418–428). Routledge.

The Global Esports Federation. (2021, March 22). Global esports federation and UNESCO to team Up: Fuelling transformative change in youth empowerment, wellbeing, and resilience. *Global Esports Federation.* www.globalsports.org/post/gef-unesco_teamup

Hayday, E. J., Collison, H., & Kohe, G. Z. (2021). Landscapes of tension, tribalism, and toxicity: Configuring a spatial politics of eSport communities. *Leisure Studies, 40*(2), 139–153. https://doi.org/10.1080/02614367.2020.1808049

Hennick, C. (2020, March 30). As esports make their way into schools, educators are seeing social and academic benefits for disengaged students. *ED Tech.* https://edtechmagazine.com/k12/article/2020/03/academic-social-boosts-show-esports-are-more-just-games

Kim, S. J. (2017). *Gender inequality in eSports participation: Examining league of legends* (Doctoral dissertation). The University of Texas. https://repositories.lib.utexas.edu/handle/2152/62914

Lee, J. Y. D., & Chou, W. H. W. (2021). Art education in eSports: How to incorporate aesthetics into the eSport marketing curriculum. In *Handbook of research on pathways and opportunities into the business of esports* (pp. 222–238). IGI Global.

Loat, R. (2021). Levelling up: Opportunities for sport for development to evolve through eSport. *Journal of Sport for Development, 9*(1), 65–73.

Peachey, J. W., Bruening, J., Lyras, A., Cohen, A., & Cunningham, G. B. (2015). Examining social capital development among volunteers of a multinational sport-for-development event. *Journal of Sport Management, 29*(1), 27–41. https://doi.org/10.1123/JSM.2013-0325

Playing for the Planet Alliance. (2021). *Empowering the games industry to play for the planet.* Playing for the Planet. https://playing4theplanet.org/

Madden, D., Liu, Y., Yu, H., Sonbudak, M. F., Troiano, G. M., & Harteveld, C. (2021, May). "Why are you playing games? You are a girl!": Exploring gender biases in esports. In *Proceedings of the 2021 CHI conference on human factors in computing systems* (pp. 1–15).

Martončik, M. (2015). e-Sports: Playing just for fun or playing to satisfy life goals? *Computers in Human Behavior, 48,* 208–211. https://doi.org/10.1016/j.chb.2015.01.056

Nicholson, J. (2021, January 12). Women in eSports joins forces with Rix.GG for VALORANT tournament. *Esports Insider.* https://esportsinsider.com/2021/01/women-in-esports-rix-gg-partnership/

Rogstad, E. T. (2021). Gender in eSports research: A literature review. *European Journal for Sport and Society,* 1–19. https://doi.org/10.1080/16138171.2021.1930941

Saeed, S., Fletcher, B., Gowers, R., & Csizmadia, A. (2018). *Esports: Engaging education.* Digital School House. www.digitalschoolhouse.org.uk/media/Documents-and-reports/Esports-Engaging-Education-SCREEN.pdf

Samples, R. (2019, April 12). New York excelsior teams up with kids in the game to bring esports to middle schools. *Dotesports.* https://dotesports.com/general/news/nyxl-kids-in-the-game-bring-esports-to-middle-schools

Shaw, A. (2012). Do you identify as a gamer? Gender, race, sexuality, and gamer identity. *New Media & Society, 14*(1), 28–44. https://doi.org/10.1177/1461444811410394

Sherry, E., Schulenkorf, N., & Chalip, L. (2015). Managing sport for social change: The state of play. *Sport Management Review, 18*(1), 1–5. https://doi.org/10.1016/j.smr.2014.12.001

Smith, D. (2020, September 28). The biggest gaming companies from around the world formed an alliance one year ago to combat climate change. Its architect explains how video games can save the planet. *Business Insider.* www.businessinsider.com/playing-for-the-planet-alliance-trista-patterson-playmob-sony-2020-9?r=US&IR=T

Reames, M. (2018, June 21). *The overlap between STEM education and esports.* SportsTechie. www.sporttechie.com/stem-esports-league-of-legends-columbia-college-oregon-syracuse/

Trepte, S., Reinecke, L., & Juechems, K. (2012). The social side of gaming: How playing online computer games creates online and offline social support. *Computers in Human Behavior, 28,* 832–839. https://doi.org/10.1016/j.chb.2011.12.003

Wave for Change. (2021). *Surf therapy: Child-friendly mental health services for under-resourced communities.* Waves for Change. https://waves-for-change.org/

Women in Games. (2021). *Women in games WIGJ for more women in video games and esports.* Women in Games. www.womeningames.org/.

4 Esports, health, and wellbeing

Key Questions

1. *How can esports support the achievement of positive health and well-being outcomes?*
2. *What are the possible negative contributions of esports to health and wellbeing?*
3. *How can positive participation in esports be encouraged and ensured?*

Introduction

Esports have become an important part of popular culture, and therefore it is important to consider the positive and negative impacts that esports participation could have on individuals and their wellbeing. Research has indicated that online gaming can result in multiple negative health effects and therefore, concerns and questions have been posed around the potential for gaming disorders and addiction (Kelly & Leung, 2021; Mihara & Higuchi, 2017; Taylor, 2018). Alongside the negative consequences of esports participation that need to be mitigated against, there is potential for esports to be used to support health, wellbeing, and social outcomes. A recently published study suggests heavier gaming participation is likely to result in higher wellbeing risks, while moderate gaming was found to be less risky and displays some positive benefits (Kelly et al., 2021). Studies have associated gaming disorders with negative social behaviours and isolation, whilst others have reported online gaming can enhance social networks and friendships, resulting in calls to examine how esports could be leveraged to "promote connectivity and social cohesion among youth in socially isolated communities" for example (Kelly & Leung, 2021, p. 8).

This chapter explores how esports can positively and negatively impact health and wellbeing for all involved. As an industry in its infancy there is currently limited evidence in relation to its health impacts, however case studies and

DOI: 10.4324/9781003213598-4

examples of regulation and initiatives newly implemented respond to the current health and wellbeing landscape within esports participation. Virtual environments and deep routed esports cultures have created a melting pot of toxic behaviour and the implications of these negative and sometimes discriminatory practices, will be further discussed.

Esports – is it addictive?

Key health organisations have differing perspectives on the nature and risks associated with esports and online gaming, with the World Health Organisation (2021) listing 'Gaming Disorder' as a mental disorder characterised by a pattern of persistent behaviour evidenced by:

a) impaired control over gaming (e.g., onset, frequency, intensity, duration, termination, context).
b) increasing priority given to gaming to the extent that gaming takes precedence over other life interests and daily activities.
c) continuation or escalation of gaming despite the occurrence of negative consequences.

The American Psychiatric Association (APA) has recognised 'Internet Gaming Disorder' and identified that gaming must cause significant distress or impairment in multiple aspects of an individuals life to be classified as gaming disorder (American Psychiatric Association, 2018). Academic research has highlighted concerns surrounding gaming disorders, which have been associated with numerous other mental health concerns such as anxiety and depression (Adams et al., 2019; Mihara & Higuchi, 2017). However existing research into this phenomenon has focused more broadly on online gaming, rather than esports, resulting in calls for further research focusing on the physical, mental health, and social impact of esports specifically (Kelly & Leung, 2021). Another complexity with comparing evidence to understand the potential health and wellbeing risks is the wider ranging definition used for gaming, dangerous gaming and gaming disorder that may extend beyond esports, to more general screen time, for example. This coupled with the measures of addiction which are difficult to assess reliably, adds complexity when looking to fully understand the positive and negative wellbeing implications of esports. The publication of the APA mental disorders manual did begin to make things clearer, as this provided a set of criteria and characteristics through which gaming disorder could be measured (Griffiths et al., 2015).

Although there is no global or universal consensus on the addictive characteristics of online gaming, Chung et al. (2019) identified increased demand for treatment provision to support gaming disorder and addiction, and some nations have identified excessive gaming as a major public health issue. Specifically, the Chinese Government started regulating the gaming industry in 2018, implementing an age-restriction system, limiting game time, and regulating the number of new online games in response to concerns for the wellbeing and health youth populations (BBC News, 2018). Proactive action has also been taken by video game publishers, Tencent (the world's largest gaming company) including enforced monitoring systems into games to require age and identity to be verified by state records. Such actions, taken at national and organisational levels, highlight the awareness and concerns key stakeholders have regarding the possible negative health and social cultures of gaming addiction seen within esports. However, have these actions been enough?

This strong governmental intervention illustrates one approach to addressing concerns around online gaming and the frequency in which youth populations are participating. Compounding this risk, is the depth of engagement in gaming in terms of duration, which some research suggesting that for gamers over 18 the global average is 8.45 hours of gaming per week (Clement, 2021). Despite these measures at a national level, the impact of these restrictions on playing freedom is unclear, given the important role that esports plays in many individuals' lives, and the positive effects competitive gaming has on social connectivity, communication, cognitive spatial awareness, and decision-making (Boyle et al., 2011; Halbrook et al., 2019). Esports provide many individuals with a sense of community and belonging, alongside opportunities of social interaction, development of social capital and cognitive skills, so is removing that outlet the most realistic solution?

Esports – virtually booming in 'lockdown' – building global communities

The COVID-19 pandemic has accelerated the growth of esports with global increases seen both in participation and streaming rates. Esports have provided a mechanism for people to socialise safely, during a period when many governments enforced extended lockdowns, and restrictions on social interaction and mobility. With many sectors (sport, theatre, hospitality) temporarily halted, individuals looked for forms of entertainment and connection from home. Esports offered a dynamic, fun, and competitive option unaffected by physical restrictions, due to its virtual nature. The alignment with traditional sports in terms of competitive intensity, sports genres, and socialisation also offered a safe and attractive replacement to live sporting events during the pandemic. Through digital spaces individuals were brought together through their shared passion for a specific esports title and this offered a mechanism for people to interact and communicate freely without limits. Isolation and subsequent loneliness resulted in significant mental health implications during the pandemic, but esports brought individuals together and offered a sense of belonging, community, and support at a time many needed it most (Langille et al., 2020).

Esports' potential to support social outcomes was covered in detail in the previous chapter (Chapter 3) exposing the valuable and important role that esports can play in supporting wellbeing and social outcomes, as part of popular culture. Yet a paradox exists with regards to esports engagement. As an activity, esports are designed to be addictive through their ability to hook users, creating an appetite for repeated engagement. Yet, this creates complexity when considering the risks and benefits that esports provide. Although esports can be a pleasurable recreational activity and a core driver of identity. However, there are notable concerns regarding negative consequences of esports in relation to health and wellbeing that must be considered.

Esports and mental wellbeing

Unprecedented growth and interest in esports have resulted in heightened focus on mental wellbeing and specifically on how mental health concerns within esports can be supported and mitigated. At the elite level, countless professional athletes have already left the esports scene due to injury, pain and stress (Shulze et al., 2021). For example, esports athlete Jian Zihao, arguably one of China's most famous esports athletes, retired aged 23. Famous for competing in League of Legends, under the name of 'Uzi', he announced his decision to retire on Chinese social media site Weibo, stating "as a result of staying up late for years, a fatty diet, and being under insurmountable stress, last year I found out that I was type-2 diabetic" (BBC News, 2020). Even with an adapted work schedule, increased exercise, and medication the situation didn't improve, and Jian said, "my mental state is not as good as it was before", and he therefore made the decision to end his career in his early 20s to focus on his health (BBC News, 2020). This is an example of how popular culture, esports, addiction, and health collide, with potentially serious consequences.

Unlike many industries, where in their 20s individuals are unlikely to fully establish themselves as they are just starting their careers, professional esports athletes are often nearing retirement. The demands of playing professional esports are stressful physically, emotionally, and mentally, with training often being undertaken daily for over ten hours a day. The high intensity training regime means that stress and burn out are a common reality for young professional athletes within the esports sector. Action is being taken and partnerships are being formed to address the impact of these stresses, for example, between game publisher Riot Games and mental health charity Active Minds, who are now showcasing prioritisation of mental wellbeing and healthy gaming practices (Koh, 2020). Research by Miah (2020) examined 70 esports companies to better understand how esports organisations support the wellness of their esports communities and discovered varied approaches, often reactive in nature, with some examples of best practice. Yet holistically there was limited continuity or monitoring in place, resulting in calls for an online esports player management system, reflecting the complexity of the fractured esports system.

With the professionalisation of the sector, esports organisations are recognising the importance and need to support player welfare and wellbeing, with specific polices, strategies and programmes being implemented to address these concerns. At an international level, the Global Esports Federation (GEF) commitment to holistic health within esports, has led to the creation of the 'education, culture and wellness' commission. The commission comprises of global experts, academics and role models who will promote optimised performance, wellbeing, and a balanced lifestyle (Global Esports Federation, 2021). Specialist support services are being incorporated into the provision for elite esports teams, with psychologists being brought in to support players, and in some cases staff, such as Misfits Gaming Group who are prioritising wellbeing and culture by offering support and mental health services across the whole workforce (Stubbs, 2021). The next case study provides a reflection from esports director Kalvin Chung, at MNM Gaming (a successful UK esports team), which shows the growing responsibility and needs for organisational intervention to support health and wellbeing.

Case Study: Reflective Piece: Kalvin Chung, Esports Director at MNM Gaming

The Importance of Health and Wellbeing: Management Perspective of an Esports Team

> *"Management looked to . . . control various aspects of the working environment which was previously messy and unclear and negatively impacted the mental health and wellbeing of esports athletes."*

Health and wellbeing are key for any country, industry, firm, team, family, and individual and that is no different for the esports space. Esports was built from passion, community, and competition where none could have imagined how quickly the industry would grow which subsequently caused many problems for both athletes and teams.

Mental health suffered greatly due to a lack of separation from work and personal life as gaming houses became an economical way for teams to achieve better results. Gaming houses were mostly residential houses which had all the athletes and management living and training together under one roof. In the MNM Gaming Leicester gaming house in 2017, the athletes found it difficult to find their own space to reflect, relax, and reset. Young athletes who had not yet experienced such personal working environments found it difficult to effectively communicate and it is not uncommon to hear of quarrels and relationships breaking down in this environment.

The surge in investments coupled with past learnings resulted in the economical need of gaming houses being a thing of the past. Offices, chefs, nutritionists, psychologists, and scheduled working hours all looked to restructure the work life balance of esports athletes and staff. Set working hours put the work back into the hands of the management, where previously athletes would argue whether their teammates were practicing enough. This is one example where management looked to reign in and control various aspects of the working environment which was previously messy and unclear and negatively impacted the mental health and wellbeing of esports athletes. Structured hours also allowed more time for physical fitness and more healthy diets.

People are at the core of esports, and it is understandable that athletes, who previously held a lot of the power and decision making in team environments and practices, were unwilling to accept the transition from what they knew in a community feel gaming house to a more structured and corporate environment. However, I believe the current world-class teams have adapted well in keeping the spirit of esports in a more corporate environment to better the health, lifestyle, and wellbeing of athletes and staff.

Alongside mental health, physical activity is recognised as a driver of physical health but can also support psychological wellbeing and this must be considered within the esports sector. Esports by its very nature can be attributed to large periods of sedentary behaviour, leading to calls for health promotion strategies (Trotter et al., 2020).

Physical activity and esports

Esports is in many cases less physically demanding than most traditional sports, yet esports do require physical skill. To ensure success at the elite level, esports athletes are required to have quick reflexes, exceptional visuomotor coordination, elicit coordinative motor skills, and display body control and position endurance (Hilvoorde & Pot, 2016; Rambusch et al., 2017; Rosell Llorens, 2017). Even though physical skill is required, the sedentary nature of esports have raised concerns, especially for professional esports teams and players, who through their training are sitting for long time periods daily and endure prolonged screen time. These are acknowledged as risk factors for numerous chronic diseases, resulting in esports players being identified as a high-risk group that requires health promotion (Rudolf et al., 2020).

Trotter et al. (2020) surveyed 1,772 international esports participants across five esports and all skill levels and found that most esports players did not meet global physical activity guidelines and there were concerns around obesity for a small minority, raising serious concerns for the future health of esports players. The question around causality remains, as although increased screen time has been associated with unhealthy practices and obesity in adults, the specific link between video gaming and obesity is not strongly established (Ballard et al., 2009; Trotter et al., 2020; Marker et al., 2019). Conversely, a study undertaken in 2019 interviewed over 1,200 German esports amateurs and professionals and examined health behaviours and identified that esports participants are becoming more active. Specifically, 80% of all respondents met or exceeded the WHO's exercise recommendations of 2.5 hours per week (eSportwissen.de, 2020). Therefore, variation and disparities globally can be seen in the levels of physical activity undertaken by individuals who engage in esports at different levels, supporting the need for future research.

Proactive action has been taken by some esports stakeholders. Excel Esports which competes in Fortnite and League of Legends are arguably one of the UK's most prolific esports teams. They published a white paper as part of their 'Gaming for Better' strategy. The paper first focuses on the importance of wellbeing and lifestyle of a professional gamer by illustrating how positive participation can be supported to mitigate risks (Excel Esports, 2020). Critically, aligning with the messaging in this paper, they recommend that esports should not be seen as a replacement for physical activity, but rather a form of digital entertainment that needs to be accompanied by prescribed levels of physical activity. The virtual nature of esports spaces results in other considerations that could impact wellbeing. A common rhetoric within esports revolves around the toxic culture associated with online spaces, which may result in negative and potentially damaging experiences for individuals involved in esports, across all levels.

Toxicity in esports environments

Toxicity has various definitions, however, holistically it is categorised as a range of behaviours that create a hostile and unfriendly environment. There are many forms and types of toxicity that can be displayed in online spaces. One example is 'flaming', which is a hostile interaction that involves insulting messages and communication between users. In contrast to traditional sports which are played in person, esports online format offers anonymised environments. These are not only difficult to regulate, but also increase the chance of exposure to negative behaviour, as the virtual space affords a mirage of protection fuelling the use of negative and offensive language. Esports content creators, streamers, and professional players are subjected to a myriad of behaviours, as the communication mechanisms through esports streaming platforms (video and text chat) provide direct interaction among users. Toxic cultures are bleeding into other association forums and social platforms as well, further exacerbating the issue (Almerekhi et al., 2019).

Yet, various individuals also find online games and virtual environments a space for healthy social interaction, alongside the development of teamwork, decision making and cognitive spatial skill development. Healthy relationships are usually formed through gamers' experiences, but this is often felt alongside harmful and offensive content (e.g., discrimination, insults, sexual, or racial slurs). Toxic culture has become acknowledged as part of online gaming culture (Cote, 2021), resulting in many female gamers purposely choosing gender neutral or masculine avatars and names to avoid bullying. In the largely self-regulated esports landscape, the responsibility has been placed on game publishers to better regulate and monitor toxic gaming culture, and action is starting to be seen, with the development of the Fair Play Alliance (Fair Play Alliance, 2021). This aims to create healthy communities in online spaces and generate initiatives to monitor online toxicity through voice chat moderation tools. For example, the voice chat record and review policy on Valorant by Riot Games was recently announced (Riot Games, 2021):

> We know disruptive behavior using our voice chat is a concern for a lot of players . . . for us to take action against players who use voice comms to harass others, use hate speech, or otherwise disrupt your experience, we need to know what those players are saying. . . . We're updating our Privacy Notice to allow us to record and evaluate voice comms when a report for disruptive behavior is submitted, starting with Valorant.

Toxicity and specifically sexist behaviours towards females is a current issue facing the esports industry, as deep-rooted cultures, gender stereotypes, and hypermasculinity often result in hostile environments for women and girls within esports spaces. This culture of gender discrimination has been seen in broader video gaming and through events such as GamerGate, which highlights the derogatory treatment of women within online gaming spaces. #GamerGate originated as a counter movement to toxic, personal attacks aimed as game developer Zoe Quinn who was harassed online. Mortensen's (2018, p. 796) research into GamerGate identified the "protectiveness of the male space of video gaming", by projecting defensive, hypermasculine behaviours within esports communities. Real-world gender stigmas have influenced the uptake and the diversity of esports participation, with toxic behaviours and language being directed towards non-male, ethnic, and minority players (Ruvalcaba et al., 2018; Taylor, 2017). Therefore, through the next case study, empirical research has been undertaken to examine the different types of user behaviour present on stream chats during First Person Shooter (FPS) tournaments. This includes specific attention on the difference in treatment aimed towards male and female athletes to help understand the level and types of toxicity targeted to specific genders.

Case Study: Exploring levels of toxicity in tournament stream chats – First Person Shooter analysis of four matches (By Kishan Radia – MSc student Institute for Sport Business, Loughborough London)

Four esports matches and the subsequent stream chats were analysed (North America (NA) one male and one female, European two all-male) teams. Thirty minutes' worth of comments from each stream chat were coded and categorised into positive, negative, or neutral language, as shown in Tables 4.1 and 4.2. Research was conducted between June and September 2021.

Results highlight that neutral (63%) comments dominated all analysed streams, followed by negative (20%), and positive (17%) comments (Table 4.1). Specific differences were found when comparing the North American all-male and all-female matches, with the all-female match stream chat showcasing significantly more positive comments than the all-male chat (Table 4.2), which may indicate that positive behaviours could be acting as a counter measure to address negative behaviours. Critically, the all-male match although displaying higher levels of negative comments, had less instances of comments that fell into discriminatory or insults sub-category, which could suggest that even though the frequency was less within the female match the type of negative comments were more harmful (Table 4.2). Example of negative comments from both matches can be seen in Table 4.3.

Table 4.1 Percentage breakdown of comments per category and sub-category across all four stream chats analysed with examples

Category	Sub-category	Behaviour	Examples
Negative (20%)	Discriminatory (2.3%)		"Kitchen goooo . . ."
		Gender or Sexism	
		Health and Disability	
		Racial	
	General (37.4%)		"Get me in the server i can miss that shot too"
		Boredom	
		Irony and Sarcasm	
		Trolling or Mockery	
	Insults (18.8%)		"EU teams trash"
		Chat Wars	
		Cursing, Profanity or Exclusionary	
		Regional Insult	
	Personal (0.75%)		"Where is the dudes chin?"
		Appearance	
		Sexual	
	Spam (40.1%)		"Absolute Slaughter"
		Negative Spam	
		Toxic Copypasta	

(Continued)

Table 4.1 (Continued)

Category	Sub-category	Behaviour	Examples
Neutral (63%)	Current Match or Stream (80.7%)		"Who won the first match?"
		Emojis Match Discussion Stream Discussion Technical Messages	
	Other (10.8%)		"*Player* is actually Drake"
		Different Mode (Emoji or Spam) Neutral Copypasta Off-topics or Current Events	
	Personal (8.5%)		"Why is *Player* not blinking o_o"
		Appearance Player description	
Positive (17%)	Challenging Negativity (1.8%)		"Being someone's fan is okay, but why hatred for the other?"
		Challenging Negativity	
	Excitement (6.4%)		"WOW"
		Amazement or Delight Excitement Greeting or Partying	
	Personal (9.9%)		*Player* is GOAT, love to see it"
		Appearance Praise Sadness (Empathy)	
	Spam (81.9%)		"POGGG"
		Positive Spam (100%)	

Table 4.2 Comparison of comments between all-male and all-female North American matches

Category	Sub-Category	NA Male Match	NA Female Match
Negative	Total (Negative)	22.70%	15.71%
	Discriminatory	1.75%	11.81%
	General	47.95%	44.65%
	Personal	18.52%	15.87%
	Insults	0.19%	0.37%
	Spam	31.58%	27.31%
Neutral	Total (Neutral)	64.20%	62.84%
Positive	Total (Positive)	13.10%	21.45%

Table 4.3 Example of negative comments from the all-male and all-female North American matches

Sub-Category	NA Male match examples
Discriminatory	Is he a male pre-2020 era?
General	gg *Team* throwing for food:(
Insults	daps pu55y
Spam	JUST FF LUL

Sub-Category	NA Female match examples
Discriminatory	why tf do they have woman teams
General	what am i watching?
Insults	*Player* is good, but so cocky and slimy it's actually annoying
Spam	post plant cringe post plant cringe post plant cringe

Overall, this research showcases that the levels of toxicity and specifically, the disparity of treatment between male and female professional players is a key issue at elite levels and may require continued monitoring and consideration of how best to minimise these behaviours within online gaming spaces.

Toxic practices and behaviours within online gaming spaces are established and deep-rooted and key industry stakeholders are currently grappling with suitable approaches to try and reduce the impact of these negative behaviours. Critically, this is something that needs to be supported and advocated for at an organisational level, but also needs to be encouraged and policed (as we are seeing) by esports communities themselves. Looking at the future of the esports industry there are numerous growth areas which can act as trigger points for health and wellbeing concerns, and one important consideration is gambling, due to its addictive and potentially damaging nature.

Harmful product advertising in esports

Globally, the esports betting market was estimated to be worth $30 billion in 2020 and its growth has been accelerated by increased COVID-19 pandemic participation and growth. In the UK for example, bookmakers such as Betway and Bet365, are capitalising on esports tournaments and adding it to their roster of betting offerings. This explosive growth has been fuelled by an increase in online advertising of esports gambling, which is mainly promoted through social media platforms. Unlike traditional sport gambling, betting operators are marketing in creative ways to promote esports betting (using memes, gifs, funny images related to the game and game specific knowledge) rather than using more impulsive, direct advertising through free bets and sign-up incentives. This is resulting in heightened engagement from younger, potentially vulnerable individuals, who are being drawn towards negative behaviours, such as gambling or alcohol (Kelly &Van der Leij, 2020). Chapter 2 outlined the fundamental components of esports gambling, yet negative product advertising is not limited to gambling, alcohol, junk food, and energy drinks. The prevalence of exposure to harmful product advertising and linked to preference and behaviour (Kelly & Van der Leij, 2020).

Within the gambling industry creative marketing strategies employed by betting companies have resulted in users who are significantly below 18 years, for which gambling is illegal in the UK (Rossi & Nairn, 2020). Underaged gamblers and betting cultures targeting youth populations could have significant implications for the wellbeing and future behaviours of young individuals who esports organisations have a duty of care to as minors.

Gambling acts as a trigger for wellbeing concerns within the esports ecosystem, as it is designed to entice and hook individuals into this potentially negative, addictive practice. The average age of gamblers is decreasing, and in 2019 17% of UK esports gamblers were aged between 18–24. This adds to the need for caution when considering the impact of gambling on the largely unregulated esports sector. The 'Young People and Gambling' report undertaken in 2019[1] identified the rise of 11–16-year-olds who gamble regularly, with 50,000 children being identified as problem gamblers, leading to a major welfare concern. This report resulted in calls to tighten regulations on esports betting advertising, as many young individuals have been exposed to gambling through smart phone apps and loot boxes in online games.

Blurred lines between esports and casinos

Traditional casinos are looking for innovative ways to reach new audiences and younger gamblers, making esports an attractive proposition. Collaborations between casinos and the esports industry suggest blurred lines between the competitive video gaming space and other gaming/gambling formats. For many, Las Vegas is the home of gambling and in 2017 a dedicated esports arena opened, HyperX Esports Arena which is based at the Luxor Hotel & Casino. The Las Vegas esports arena experience made a statement about the future directions and relationship between gambling and esports. This is driven by the commercial motivation of the sector stemming from private ownership. Sponsorship is also an area where many deals between esports organisations, sports betting sites and casinos have been seen. For example the partnership between Betway and esports organisation Ninjas in Pyjamas, or the casino sponsorship between Complexity Gaming and Win Star Casino (Esports Insider, 2021). Whilst the title of this section suggests blurred lines between esports gambling cultures and casinos, the evidence suggests that the lines are becoming more distinct, and gambling is fast becoming an embedded feature of the esports sector that could have long-term wellbeing effects in the future.

Overall, the opportunities and potential for commercialisation (advertising and sponsorship) within esports is endless, yet there is a need to consider the implications for vulnerable user groups who are attracted and likely to partake in such activity. Calls for tighter regulation and governance have been proposed, as discussed in Chapter 2. Although rules and laws are in place to protect children from participating or being targeted through advertising, there has been recognition that more needs to be done to better regulate esports marketing and protect children and young adults from its dangers. The lucrative esports industry will continue to attract interest from multiple stakeholders and as esports continue to evolve and engage wide ranging audiences, other silos of the gambling sector, such as betting operators and casinos will continue to look for new audiences to monetise. Therefore, accountability and appropriate regulation is critical to protect the wellbeing of a highly impressionable and vulnerable youth population.

Conclusion

This chapter has illustrated the multiple perspectives and ambiguous nature of health and wellbeing in the esports industry. Although a variety of claims, concerns, and considerations have been raised, we are seeing a lot of positive action being taken as this industry evolves to address and mitigate against some of the negative and potentially damaging practices. Critically, for a young industry that is evolving at a rapid pace, the impacts, both positive and negative, upon participants' wellbeing are still emerging. Recent reviews conducted by Kelly and Leung (2021) and Kelly et al. (2021) considered the health consequences (physical, lifestyle, cognitive, mental, or social). Importantly those reviews highlighted the paucity of empirical research into esports and the associated positive and negative health and wellbeing outcomes, with further research needing to account for the different forms of participation in esports. Kelly et al. (2021) carried out a cross sectional survey of Australian gamers and non-gamers aged between 12 and 24 years and their parents. Heavy gaming was associated with adverse health consequences, compared to light/casual gaming. This indicates that mitigation strategies targeting moderate engagement could be effective, specifically parental interventions linked to gaming time limits, expectations around physical activity contributed to whether a minor was a causal or heavy gamer (Kelly et al., 2021). This sheds light on current esports behaviours and possible mitigation strategies that could contribute to positive engagement in esports.

This chapter has shown that across a myriad of health and wellbeing considerations, esports can support both positive outcomes but can also lead to negative consequences. Therefore, with esports' growing popularity, it is important to explore and identify how positive wellbeing outcomes can be leveraged, and risks minimised or countered. Case studies and examples throughout this chapter have showcased that health and wellbeing is a key consideration in the esports industry with multiple mechanisms being created and implemented to enhance the credibility of the industry and support positive participation in esports. There is no doubt that the fractured nature of the industry is adding to the complexity of tackling some of these challenges, yet we are seeing a cultural shift both internally, as esports stakeholders identify the importance and responsibility to support the health and wellbeing of its community, but also externally as key organisations start to realise the potential of esports to support different development agendas. For example, we see an unlikely ally in the form of the WHO, create an initiative #PlayApartTogether, in collaboration with several esports gaming industry leaders (Sanchez, 2021) during the COVID-19 pandemic. The initiative disseminated important health guidelines relevant to the crisis such as hand washing, social distancing, and staying home, by promoting gaming at home as a safe way to connect with others. This is a significant shift in perspective by the WHO, who have previously raised health concerns suggesting that online gaming was 'addictive'; yet during the pandemic they acknowledged esports function as an important social connection mechanism. Therefore, if influential organisations such as the WHO, which historically have opposed and rejected the esports space, now acknowledge its potential, there are countless opportunities here. This offers an outlet for knowledge sharing between sectors to enhance the regulations and welfare support for the bourgeoning esports industry, whilst importantly illustrating the limitless possibilities for esports to be used as a hook for development outcomes.

Note

1 Subsequent years' data and sample sizes were heavily impacted by COVID-19 and school closures.

References

Adams, B. L., Stavropoulos, V., Burleigh, T. L., Liew, L. W., Beard, C. L., & Griffiths, M. D. (2019). Internet gaming disorder behaviors in emergent adulthood: A pilot study examining the interplay between anxiety and family cohesion. *International Journal of Mental Health and Addiction, 17*(4), 828–844. https://doi.org/10.1007/s11469-018-9873-0

Almerekhi, H., Kwak, H., Jansen, B. J., & Salminen, J. (2019, September). Detecting toxicity triggers in online discussions. In *Proceedings of the 30th ACM Conference on Hypertext and Social Media*. (pp. 291-292).

American Psychiatric Association. (2018, June). *Internet gaming*. American Psychiatric Association. www.psychiatry.org/patients-families/internet-gaming

Ballard, M., Gray, M., Reilly, J., & Noggle, M. (2009). Correlates of video game screen time among males: Body mass, physical activity, and other media use. *Eating Behaviours, 10*(3), 161–167. doi:10.1016/j.eatbeh.2009.05.001

BBC News. (2018, August 31). China targets video gaming to tackle myopia in children. *BBC News*. www.bbc.co.uk/news/world-asia-china-45366468

BBC News. (2020, June 4). Gaming 'hero' retires at 23 due to ill-health. *BBC News*. www.bbc.co.uk/news/technology-52920786

Boyle, E., Connolly, T. M., & Hainey, T. (2011). The role of psychology in understanding the impact of computer games. *Entertainment Computing, 2*(2), 69–74. https://doi.org/10.1016/j.entcom.2010.12.002

Chung, T., Sum, S., Chan, M., Lai, E., & Cheng, N. (2019). Will esports result in a higher prevalence of problematic gaming? A review of the global situation. *Journal of Behavioral Addictions, 8*(3), 384–394. doi:10.1556/2006.8.2019.46

Clement, J. (2021, April 23) Weekly hours spent playing video games worldwide 2021, by country, *Statista*. https://www.statista.com/statistics/273829/average-game-hours-per-day-of-video-gamers-in-selected-countries/

Cote, A. (2021, August 21). Here's what it'll take to clean up esports' toxic culture. *The Conversation*. https://theconversation.com/heres-what-itll-take-to-clean-up-esports-toxic-culture-143520

Esports Insider. (2021, May 26). The growing link between esports betting and casinos. *Esports Insider*. https://esportsinsider.com/2021/05/the-growing-link-between-esports-betting-and-casinos/

eSportwissen.de. (2020). Esports study 2020-wellbeing and recovery. *Esportwissen.* www.esportwissen.de/en/esport-studie-2020-gesundheit-und-erholung-von-esportlern/

Excel Esports. (2020, November 12). Gaming for better: Whitepaper. *Excel Esports.* https://xl.gg/blogs/news/gaming-for-better

Fair Play Alliance. (2021). *Together for fair play.* Fair Play Alliance. https://fairplayalliance.org/

Global Esports Federation. (2021, February 18). The global esports federation expands commitment to health and wellness in esports. *Global Esports.* www.globalesports.org/post/health-and-wellness-in-esports

Griffiths, M. D., Király, O., Pontes, H. M., & Demetrovics, Z. (2015). An overview of problematic gaming. In E. Aboujaoude & V. Starcevic (Eds.), *Mental health in the digital age: Grave dangers, great promise* (pp. 27–45). Oxford University Press.

Halbrook, Y. J., O'Donnell, A. T., & Msetfi, R. M. (2019). When and how video games can be good: A review of the positive effects of video games on wellbeing. *Perspectives on Psychological Science, 14*(6), 1096–1104. https://doi.org/10.1177/1745691619863807

Hilvoorde, I. V., & Pot, N. (2016). Embodiment and fundamental motor skills in eSports. *Sport, Ethics and Philosophy, 10*(1), 14–27. https://doi.org/10.1080/17511321.2016.1159246

Kelly, S. J., & Leung, J. (2021). The new frontier of esports and gaming: A scoping meta-review of health impacts and research agenda. *Frontiers in Sports and Active Living, 3*, 1–10. https://doi.org/10.3389/fspor.2021.640362

Kelly, S. J., Magor, T., & Wright, A. (2021). The pros and cons of online competitive gaming: An evidence-based approach to assessing young players' well-being. *Frontiers in Psychology, 12*, 1–9. https://doi.org/10.3389/fpsyg.2021.651530

Kelly, S. J., & Van der Leij, D. (2020). A new frontier: Alcohol sponsorship activation through esports. *Marketing Intelligence & Planning, 39*(4), 533–558. https://doi.org/10.1108/MIP-03-2020-0101

Koh, S. M. (2020, March 6). LCS partners with mental health organization active minds. *Riot Games.* www.riotgames.com/en/who-we-are/social-impact/lcs-partners-with-mental-health-organization-active-minds

Langille, A., Daviau, C., & Hawreliak, J. (2020, April 1). Playing video games can ease loneliness during the coronavirus pandemic. *The Conversation.* https://theconversation.com/playing-video-games-can-ease-loneliness-during-the-coronavirus-pandemic-134198

Marker, C., Gnambs, T., & Appel, M. (2019). Exploring the myth of the chubby gamer: A meta-analysis on sedentary video gaming and body mass. *Social Science and Medicine*, 1–9. https://doi.org/10.1016/j.socscimed.2019.05.030

Miah, A. (2020). How do esports companies support their community's wellness? *International Journal of Esports, 1*, 1–12. www.ijesports.org/article/18/html

Mihara, S., & Higuchi, S. (2017). Cross-sectional and longitudinal epidemiological studies of internet gaming disorder: A systematic review of the literature. *Psychiatry and Clinical Neurosciences, 71*(7), 425–444. doi:10.1111/pcn.12532

Mortensen, T. E. (2018). Anger, fear, and games: The long event of# GamerGate. *Games and Culture, 13*(8), 787–806. doi:10.1177/1555412016640408

Rambusch, J., Taylor, A. S. A., & Susi, T. (2017). *Cognitive challenges in esports*. Proceedings of the 13 Swecog Conference 2017, UPPSALA. www.diva-portal. org/smash/get/diva2:1156189/FULLTEXT01.pdf#page=65]

RiotGames.(2021,April30).News:Updatingtheprivacynoticeandtermsofservice.*Riot Games*. www.riotgames.com/en/news/updating-the-privacy-notice-and-terms-of-service

Rosell Llorens, M. (2017). Esport gaming: The rise of a new sports practice. *Sport, Ethics and Philosophy*, *11*(4), 464–476. https://doi.org/10.1080/17511321.2017. 1318947

Rossi, R., & Nairn, A. (2020, October 1). Esports could be quietly spawning a whole new generation of problem gamblers. *The Conversation*. https://theconversation. com/esports-could-be-quietly-spawning-a-whole-new-generation-of-problem-gamblers-147124

Rudolf, K., Bickmann, P., Froböse, I., Tholl, C., Wechsler, K., & Grieben, C. (2020). Demographics and health behavior of video game and eSports players in Germany: The esports study 2019. *International Journal of Environmental Research and Public Health*, *17*(6), 1870. doi:10.3390/ijerph17061870

Ruvalcaba, O., Shulze, J., Kim, A., Berzenski, S. R., & Otten, M. P. (2018). Women's experiences in esports: Gendered differences in peer and spectator feedback during competitive video game play. *Journal of Sport and Social Issues*, *42*(4), 295–311. https://doi.org/10.1177/0193723518773287

Sanchez, S. (2021, April 13), Gaming platforms reactivate #PlayApartTogether campaign with World Health Organization, *Campaign*. https://www.campaign-live.co.uk/article/gaming-platforms-reactivate-playaparttogether-campaign-world-health-organization/1712767

Shulze, J., Marquez, M., & Ruvalcaba, O. (2021). The Biopsychosocial Factors That Impact eSports Players' Well-Being: A Systematic Review. *Journal of Global Sport Management*, 1–25.

Stubbs, M. (2021, June 9). Why esports team misfits is prioritizing mental health for players and staff. *Forbes*. www.forbes.com/sites/mikestubbs/2021/06/09/why-esports-team-misfits-is-prioritizing-mental-health-for-players-and-staff/?sh=1aebc44158e4

Taylor, M. M. (2018). The globesity epidemic. *The Obesity Epidemic*, 1–20. doi:10.1007/978-3-319-68978-4_1

Taylor, T. L. (2017). *On the fields, in the stands: The future of women in esports* [Keynote]. Presented at the UCI esports symposium, University of California, Irvine, May 19.

Trotter, M. G., Coulter, T. J., Davis, P. A., Poulus, D. R., & Polman, R. (2020). The association between eSports participation, health, and physical activity behaviour. *International Journal of Environmental Research and Public Health*, *17*(19), 1–14. https://doi.org/10.3390/ijerph17197329

World Health Organisation. (2021, May). ICD-11 for mortality and morbidity statistics. *ICD*. https://icd.who.int/browse11/l-m/en#/http://id.who.int/icd/entity/1448597234

5   Esports evolution

Key Questions

1. *As the esports industry professionalises what does the future look like for this fast-growing sector?*
2. *Could esports be used as a 'hook' for social development outcomes?*
3. *What are the growth areas within the esports industry that will impact its evolution in the coming years?*

Esports continual growth

Continual and exponential growth is the best way to characteristic the speed at which the esports industry has originated, evolved, and is starting to stabilise. Due the dynamic, adaptive nature of the industry nothing stays the same for long. Mobile has recently been identified as a new pillar of the esports industry. Smartphone access reduces entry barriers for many individuals who do not own a console or PC, and this has significant implications for the global reach of esports. Fuelled by the popularity of free-to-play competitive games such as PUBG Mobile, in emerging markets such as India, mobile esports is an upward trend within the esports sphere (Nordland, 2021). Global market revenues from mobile esports were $875.3 million in 2021 and the growth and value of mobile esports content continues to rise (Gough, 2021).

Appetite for mobile esports is also evident with game publisher Riot Games announcing development plans for their new League of Legends mobile game Wild Rift (Sacco, 2021). Some esports titles have multiple versions, allowing the game title to be played on a console, PC, or mobile, whilst others have been made exclusively for mobile devices. This offers new expansion opportunities which will not only offer commercial revenues, but increase the reach to esports, through mobile. For emerging,

DOI: 10.4324/9781003213598-5

developing markets, such as the Global South, this may offer an entry point to esports, through the proliferation of smartphone ownership and increased levels of internet access globally.

The pace of change within the industry is not limited to the playing format, popular game titles themselves are continually challenged by new esports titles, as game developers and publishers are continually trying to keep up with the demand and appetite for new narratives and more immersive, appealing games. This often comes at a high premium for game publishers, with Epic Games for example spending $100 million developing its Fortnite esports scene (Nordland, 2021). Yet, the fragility of esports titles cultural relevance can result in their popularity diminishing as quickly as they appear. Even four years ago (early 2017) two major esports titles didn't exist, Fortnite and Valorant, suggesting that future titles that will dominate the esports landscape are likely to alter. With technological advancements, fans will be enticed by new immersive esports offerings, as the industry continues to evolve and reaches new audiences.

Diversification by traditional sports into esports

With traditional sport spectator numbers declining and viewership through interactive media platforms increasing, a new generation of consumers has emerged (Pirker, 2020). The future is immersive and interactive and COVID-19 has not only accelerated digitalisation but has resulted in traditional sports organisations having to innovate through digital spaces. Some sport organisations were already engaged with esports, but for others COVID-19 was the stimulus, due to the pausing of live sport events. This engagement with esports could be described as a form of brand extension, enabling sports to virtually connect and engage with consumers and fill content voids in the sporting calendar (Ké & Wagner, 2020). For example, in 2020, Formula One held the Esports Virtual Grand Prix series to replace their postponed races, yet its success means this has become a major pillar of Formula One's business strategy. The question remains how do the clubs that are part of professional sport leagues view the phenomenon of esports?

Through the illustrative example of the English Premier League (EPL) the next case exemplar explores if, and how, EPL clubs integrated esports into their business strategy. All EPL clubs are required to enter representative players to the ePremier League (ePL), which is an esports tournament based around the EA Sports title FIFA, facilitated by the league. The nature and extent of EPL clubs' esports activity widely varies beyond entry to the ePL.

Box 5.1

Case Study: EPL and the ePL – How are traditional sports clubs engaging with esports?

(Conducted by Toby Wilkinson – MSc student Institute for Sport Business – Loughborough London)

An analysis of 20 EPL clubs was undertaken (July–September 2021) across club websites and social media platforms to investigate how professional football clubs engaged with esports and in what ways this formed part of their brand extension strategy. Traditional sports engagement with esports was explored through two main areas:

Commercial Activity

- Any partnerships with esports/gaming companies
- Compete in/host any esports competitions or events, outside the ePL
- Engage with esports beyond football simulation

Content & Communications

- Specific esports website and/or social media pages
- Promotion of any esports rosters/players (through content and communication channels)
- Dedicated Twitch channel

Results indicate there is significant diversity in the approaches used when engaging with esports. Across a range of EPL clubs, there was no clear patterns or trends regarding the modes of engagement or specific clubs undertaking this work. Clubs are certainly experimenting, and we see various strategies and levels of esports integration across the EPL, as shown in Tables 5.1 and 5.2. Partnering with an esports or gaming organisation is the most popular way of engaging with the industry, with the implication being that clubs look to others for esports expertise. With the complexity of the esports sector, this research suggests football clubs

Table 5.1 Typology of Esports Engagement – EPL clubs 2021/22 season

Highest Esports Engagement	
Aston Villa Manchester City Watford West Ham United Wolverhampton Wanderers	Multifaceted Esports strategies covering both commercial AND content strategy.
Moderate Esports Engagement	
Arsenal Leeds United Burnley Tottenham Hotspur Norwich City Manchester United	Multiple strategies to integrate Esports into either content OR commercial activity.
Limited Esports Engagement	
Brentford Leicester City Liverpool Newcastle United Southampton Brighton & Hove Albion Chelsea Crystal Palace Everton	Limited/no Esports activity outside of ePL.

Table 5.2 Methods of engagement with esports industry for 20 EPL clubs – 2021/22 season

Commercial Activities	**60%** have partnerships with esports/gaming organisations (12/20) **35%** compete in, or host, tournaments/events/competitions, outside the ePL (7/20) **25%** engage with esports outside of football-simulation games (FIFA, PES) (5/20)
Communications and Content	**40%** have dedicated esports pages on the Club website: (8/20) **15%** have dedicated esports pages on their social media platforms (3/20) **50%** of clubs have their own Twitch channel (10/20) **30%** promote their own esports players anywhere (6/20)

are still working out the best way for them to engage, yet for many it has become a core part of their digital strategy and brand identity.

While diversification into esports is being embraced across many traditional sports, the question of whether esports will be integrated into the Olympics is currently unclear. While inclusion would resonate with young consumers and have potential to reinvigorate the Olympic brand, there are risks and strategic concerns from both esports and Olympics perspectives, which are discussed in the next section.

Inclusion in the Olympics?

The International Olympic Committee (IOC) has already recognised the commercial opportunities and popularity of esports, yet previously the IOC have been hesitant, as Esports' structures, culture, and imperatives are at odds with the values-based ethos underpinning sport (IOC, 2018). Yet, the opportunities that esports offers the IOC given its ageing audience has come to the fore, as in 2021 they outlined their plans for the Olympic Virtual Series (OVS). By partnering with five International Sports Federations (IFs) and game publishers, the OVS is the first Olympic-licensed event, including physical and non-physical virtual sports (Peters, 2021). Five sport simulation esports packaged through the OVS strenghtens the IOC's digital offering, allowing them to reach new audiences and enhance their relevance in a digitalised world. Yet, many within the esports industry would indicate this is only a small silo of what esports represents, through the focus on the sport simulation genre. The IOC are trying to keep value alignment where they can with two out of the five virtual sports requiring gamers to connect to physical hardware. This signals the IOC's attempt to keep connections between the physical and virtual realms of sport. The OVS is currently a testbed in many ways, with the IOC trialling and reflecting on the appetite for esports within this format, yet it may be possible that as early as the 2028 Los Angeles Summer Games, we might see a virtual representation of a physical sport becoming a medalled event (Peters, 2021).

Gaming culture is already proliferating the Olympic Movement. As the world tuned in for the start of the Toyoko 2020 Olympics, during the Parade of Nations, athletes were accompanied by a soundtrack full of video game references including music from Sonic the Hedgehog (Euronews, 2021). This is a specific acknowledgement of the cultural importance that gaming plays not only in Japan's history but in broader society today, and coupled with the creation of the OVS, this demonstrates the IOC's commitment to engaging with esports and its possible inclusion as a medal event in the future. Given the declining and ageing population of the Olympic Games, esports is likely to become a core pillar of the IOC's long-term business strategy, to ensure the sustainability of the Olympic Movement, by leveraging esports global popularity.

Could esports be the new 'hook' for social movements?

Chapter 3 provided an overview of esports' social value to its participants and communities and highlighted the social outcomes and impacts of competitive gaming. The opportunities for inclusive participation, enhanced social capital, and empowerment has been most notably experienced by women and girls, marginal groups and people with disabilities who have been able to form communities and engage without gendered or physical boundaries. This has not guaranteed positive experiences but esports can and does challenge many of the contested traditional barriers to participation. The social value of esports is the guiding philosophical principle that grounds community narratives promoted by esports participants.

Due to esports' unprecedented growth and usership the sector could no longer be resisted nor rejected by global development and social movements. Esports should be seen as the missing offering for many social change agendas, with the question posed by many SfD stakeholders being, how can we engage and interact with young people who do not play football or basketball or other mainstream sports? In this context, esports have been identified as a mechanism to achieve United Nations goals, reinforce social change messages, educate users on climate change and other critical issues, and support charities for social good projects.

Esports not only serves as the hook that draws in mass fandom, consumption, and transnational connectivity but also encourages the creation of new partnerships for social innovation and change. This has had positive impacts for educational offerings and growth in STEM related fields of learning and employment. The employment opportunities now created by esports-related skills and experience have grown exponentially, resulting in esports specific professional courses and qualifications, with clear trajectories into the digital and cyber innovation space. Esports' intimate relationship with entrepreneurship and innovation has acted as the vehicle for sport and social change movements that sit within a very competitive institutionalised space. Therefore, in a short period of time, esports have attracted multiple partners and alliances within education and social development sectors and this can only develop and grow with improved recognition, governance, and support. The more appropriate question may be 'why haven't more social change movements leveraged esports?' Arguably those who do not follow the cultural phenomenon will be left behind.

The rise of the esports influencer

The increase in esports popularity and commercialisation has given rise to the emergence of a new category of celebrity athlete, esports influencers. Large networks of brands are now affiliating with these influencers to capitalise on the growing reach among next generation consumers and the mainstream popularity of esports. Vast audiences for League of Legends and Fortnite Battle Royale now eclipse those of the NBA. Esports influencers may be professional athletes, but not necessarily. In fact, many casual gamers are using YouTube and Twitch platforms to connect with these audiences and are also fashion or sports influencers. For example, football player WroetoShaw[1] is also a FIFA YouTuber and GamingwithJen[2] is both a fashion and esports influencer. Commercial partnerships with influencers include brand endorsements, branded content, and product placements and testing. Influencers may extend partnerships and mentions to their broader groups, such as Taco Crew and Banana Bus Squad, which extend value beyond the immediate influencer to their groups, who are themselves often influential gamers. For example, the Banana Bus Squad includes Vanoss, Mini Lad, Moo Snuckle, and Wildcat among others, who are all popular gamers, so endorsement of one will reach all the crew's followers.

Popular influencers include VanossGaming, (Evan Fong), who is also musically and comedically talented with 25 million subscribers and 100 million monthly views, and female influencer, SSSniperwolf, (Lia Shelish), with a YouTube following of 11 million subscribers and a second YouTube following in fashion DIY (i.e., "Do it yourself" and upcycling). Influencers' audience reach can be more extensive than traditional sports or cultural influencers, with audiences following across gaming platforms, media, and social media. The highly differentiated engagement with different genres, games, and tournaments is also attractive for brands seeking to resonate with specific consumer segments. Many influencers are young and earning significant prize money and endorsements, including 16-year-old Kyle Giersdorf (Bugha) who won the Fortnite World Cup in 2019, and secured $43 million in prize money, and is now sponsored by Red Bull. To put this into perspective, the prize money awarded to 16-year-old Kyle is more than top-ranked athletes (celebrities also in their own right) often receive, with 18-year-old Emma Raducanu receiving $2.5 million in 2021 for her record-breaking U.S. Open victory (Gilchrist, 2021).

Gamers' brands are reflective of their gaming ability and their personality when commentating their playthroughs. This provides a myriad of storytelling and authentic brand engagement opportunities, along with access to a highly segmented audience across different games and genres. According to Nielsen, 24% of gamers choose to watch a streamed game based upon the host or streamer, indicating the potential for esports influencers (Nielsen, 2019). Many gaming influencers are quitting their teams and leagues to engage in full time streaming and content creation in partnership with brands. Ally Warfield, the highest ranked female gamer in the world in 2019, received an invitation to join a pro esports team, but left to pursue her own streaming and content making career, demonstrating the growing trend for gamers to migrate away from pro esports to commercialised content making and streaming.

Esports influencers are promoting positive behaviour in their young audiences. KittyPlays has established a community of gamers focussed upon positive thinking, creativity, and joy. Her community is called Team Kitty which leads a mentoring programme and network for female gamers and streamers. Hershey's recruited two of the most popular esports influencers, Lupo and Ninja, who have a combined Twitch following of 15 million and have trusted images over a long period. They co-created a mashable content piece which was livestreamed, featuring their Reese's Pieces and then cross-promoted through secondary channels including Instagram, YouTube, Twitter, in the lead up to TwitchCon in 2018 (Michelli, 2018). This campaign demonstrates successful partnering with esports influencers requires ensuring that the partner is trustworthy, as they control the dialog in a livestreaming landscape, and the need for authentic creation of the campaign or content through collaboration with influencers. Yet, given the relatively young age and high stakes placed on esports influencers, who is supporting them, their welfare, and best interests? Box 5.2 is a reflective case study written by David Yarnton, Chairperson and Co-Founder of *Edge,* he discusses the rise of esports influencers and how certain organisations such as Edge are helping to legitimise the industry by supporting influencers within the largely under regulated sector.

Case Study: The Rise of the Esports Influencer

Written by David Yarnton – Chairperson and Co-Founder of *Edge (The real-time influencer analytics platform) and founding director of Gfinity.*

There have been influencers around for a long time, I won't go back too far or include religious influence, but centuries ago people were considered influential based on their prominence within political or economic spheres, or scientific discovery (i.e., Nelson Mandela, Albert Einstein, Marie Curie). I have always felt that sometimes there isn't anything new, it's just the old, reformatted to take into consideration current technology and digitalisation. Sport in many ways created a new breed of influencers or in their time they may have been referred to as 'Trend Setters'. Fans wanted to know everything about their sporting idols (i.e., Babe Ruth, Donald Bradman, George Best, and more recently Cristiano Ronaldo). These people became famous through the medium of print, radio, and television and as the medium became more ubiquitous whatever they said or did became common knowledge globally.

Now the medium has morphed into the internet and social media is the home of the modern-day influencers, but the reach and consumption has surpassed anything imaginable from previous conduits of information. With the advent of Video Gaming and Twitch, everything now becomes Real Time in Real Life, everyone can be their own star, have their own 'Truman Show'. The new sports stars are from esports, and they have the knowledge to leverage their influence using technology beyond anything that was possible in the past. Influencers will continue to be our guidance outside of friends and family and with technology their reach is global. These new esports stars have numerous opportunities to connect to their audiences and build or in some cases destroy a brand's reputation.

As there is easy access to the internet and demand from the teams on esports players to stream on a regular basis, to promote their sponsors, the game, tournaments, and team merchandise etc., it brings new pressures to the young esports players. Apart from the time needed to practice, how do they manage all these new obligations, who educates them on media skills, who manages their connection to media agencies/brands, who makes sure they fulfil their promotional commitments, who makes sure they get paid for their efforts. Technology has created the rise of esports influencers but has not kept pace in supporting them behind the scenes. There are so many issues that esports influencers need to be aware of now and there are very few avenues available for them to be able to build their credibility through accurate data supporting their efforts and assistance in ensuring efficient payment for the fruit of their labours.

That is until now, with Edge, esports influencers can focus on creating, whilst through the support of Edge and their services influencers can be assured, they will get paid in an efficient and timely manner. As Edge's platform supports influencers by offering them a free service which offers real-time data tracking and campaign reporting across major social platforms, as well as automating influencer payments from brands and organisations for their content.

With media consumption changing among next generation young consumers, esports represents a valuable vehicle to engage typically hard-to-reach millennial and Gen Z consumers. Moreover, esports fans are particularly attractive to brands, as they are technologically savvy, often have disposable income, and stream games as spectators for an average of 100-minutes-per-session via Twitch or YouTube (Newzoo, 2021). These audiences also use ad blockers, rendering above the line advertising unsuitable, but elevating the importance of esports influencers and branded content. Mainstream brands such as Coca Cola, Red Bull, Louis Vuitton, Mercedes-Benz, Intel, and Gillette are partnering with esports through sponsorship of influencers and tournaments, infrastructure, and content.

The unique online environment of esports creates new opportunities for brand touchpoints, but there are also challenges. The interactive nature of online esports spectating differs from the more passive consumption of traditional sports and has facilitated the growth of esports influencers who can communicate brand messages and preferences via chat functions and rooms during streaming of games. Declining viewing and attendance of traditional sports among young generations has prompted sports to diversify into esports and endorse influencers in both esports and sports. The appetite and rapid growth of esports has resulted in a need for subsidiary services (such as: new tournament platforms, performance tracking systems, professional skill development, marketing agencies) to support and stabilise this bourgeoning area.

Esports and innovation – the rising esports services sector

The esports sector has attracted increasing attention from investors, brands, media outlets, and consumers, which has fuelled a proliferation of services, products, and career opportunities. The gaming basis of esports has expanded to include media, pop culture, and commerce, to evolve into an important economic and social sector. The sector experienced exponential growth in venture capital and private equity backing, with investment increasing from $497 million in 2017 to $4.5 billion in 2018, representing a growth rate of 837%, according to Deloitte (Ludwig et al., 2021). This significant investment has facilitated the further growth and maturity of the industry. Newzoo predicts that the sector will grow to $218.7 billion by 2024 (Newzoo, 2021). While traditional esports markets of Europe, Asia-Pacific, and North America continue to grow, with increasing use of mobile, accessibility to esports allows for new markets in South America and African nations. China already has a thriving mobile esports scene, which comprises round 45% of the total gaming market.

A myriad of platforms, resources, and markets exists to support the esports sector. Resources and services to support pro gamers and aspiring athletes such as coaching, statistical performance tracking, and skill enhancement technologies are growing, along with platforms and infrastructure including communication facilitation tools (e.g., Discord) and tournament platforms (e.g., Battlefy). Streaming media platforms including Twitch, YouTube, Discord, Facebook Gaming, Caffeine, and Steam TV, and associated services such as analytics and highlights are also attracting significant investment. For example, Bayes raised $6 million in 2021 to develop analytical tools for esports teams and tournaments and also distributes esports data to customers in betting, broadcasting (Takahashi, 2020). Businesses are also prevalent in the esports landscape, and there is increasing opportunity for agents, sponsorship services, and marketing services associated with esports. The franchising of esports provides further avenues for commercialisation, and demand for media, marketing, analytics, and event management skills. Gaming design and coding continue to be critical skills in the sector, and sources of innovation, including customised gaming and banded content in game.

With the prospect of employability in this high growth sector and the strong potential to attract students, colleagues are investing in the opportunity by offering esports degree programmes, short courses, and esports athletic scholarships and teams. Varsity esports training facilities are inexpensive compared to the multi-million-dollar elite training infrastructure needed in other varsity sports. For example, in the US, there are already 65 colleges running esports programmes, and there is a National Association of Collegiate Esports established in 2016, to oversee the growing collegiate competition. Inter-varsity and high school tournaments are growing rapidly, and educators are leveraging esports as a platform to better engage students in education and STEM and entrepreneurial skill-building.

Investment in esports and online gaming has been exponential, with many esports technology accelerators and venture capital funds are established globally. For example, Comcast NBCUniversal, Execution Labs, and Hype Sports Innovation have hosted esports incubators and accelerators, and Bitkraft Esports Ventures has raised $125 million for investment and incubation of esports start-ups (Ashton, 2019). In the future, mixed reality and augmented experience in gaming will provide further experiential and commercial opportunity for participants, sponsors, and the broader community to immerse in esports.

Is there a need for clearer esports regulation and governance systems?

Chapter 2 provided an overview of the challenges and opportunities for governance in esports. Esports governance is complex due to the uniquely global, digital landscape and its private ownership structures. Underlying this is a predominantly youth culture that is sceptical of authority and regulation, accompanied by publisher owners' push for self-regulation of the sector. While there are many examples of effective self-regulation by publishers, the consistency, transparency, and enforcement of policies is lacking across tournaments, leagues, and games.

Regulatory risk associated with young participants including a lack of comprehensive rights and protection in contracting, training requirements, player sanctioning, and ability to appeal decision making, have prompted the establishment of several independent organisations concerned with effective governance of the sector (Kelly et al., 2021). However, none of these independent governance models have universal jurisdiction over esports participants. External existing regulation in most jurisdictions is also largely ineffective, with esports and digital platforms failing to fall within the ambit of many definitions in anti-gambling or advertising regulations and protective codes. Gambling and advertising by harmful product categories such as alcohol and junk food are now embedded in esports yet aren't broadly regulated to protect the largely minor and young participants. Welfare issues associated with gaming addiction are also being documented, elevating the need for intervention and protection of esports participants. Gaming structure and design also needs oversight to ensure inappropriate content and latent incentives in the form of microtransactions are mitigated. It is noted that in 2021, the Chinese government implemented regulation to prevent minors gaming more than one hour per day, and restricting gameplay to weekends and public holidays (Goh, 2021). Perhaps an optimal governance model might be a hybrid of self-regulation and right to independent arbitration and oversight through national or international organisations.

Esports needs to evolve to more protectionist and effective governance to achieve mainstream recognition as a sport by international bodies including the International Olympic Committee. While the competitive intensity, popularity, and commercialisation of esports aligns with acceptance as a potential Olympic sport, its nascent governance structures do not. Positive advancement in esports governance is needed to reflect universal principles of transparency, consistency, accountability, and trust. However, any system will need to embrace youth voice and leadership to ensure that a top-down approach is avoided and that the creative and independent culture and commercial DNA of esports is preserved, while protecting vulnerable consumers.

Conclusion remarks – an optimistic future for esports

The future of esports is bright, with expected continued growth of 15% per year, audiences of almost half a billion and a sector value of approximately $1.3 billion by 2023. To bring this extraordinary growth into perspective, esports has now eclipsed audiences in professional sports and is emerging as the converging platform for music, gaming, fashion, and culture. Many esports teams and professional players have significant influence through social media and esports platforms, to a notoriously inaccessible, ad-blocking next generation market. With the last five years of esports seeing such astronomical growth and opportunity across the sector, the next decade presents exciting opportunities to further commercialise the sector and strengthen its position as a key vehicle for positive impact for its audiences, employees, and society. According to Newzoo (2021), sponsorship and partnering is expected to proliferate, as will investment in esports content, teams, and leagues. This continued influx of financial backing will be matched by increased accessibility to esports via mobile, and the consequent reach to large, young audiences in South America, India, and African nations.

Esports affiliations with established and trusted sporting brands will also build favourable esports brand image and credibility, as sports seek to create novel revenue streams and fandom through virtual branding in esports. Engagement in esports will be enhanced dramatically over the next few years, with increasing technological sophistication in gaming experience creation, viewing, and interaction. Immersive and mixed reality gaming will be the new norm, and with this, opportunity for esports to emerge as more inclusive and democratised, and leverage its decentralised, hyperconnected model. With this elevation to mainstream legitimacy, esports is well positioned to lead socially responsible initiatives that resonate with target audiences, corporate sponsors, governments, and society. Esports can unite and garner youth support and advocacy in relation to universal, wicked social issues of inequality, climate change, and access to education.

If we reflect on these frequently discussed issues: **How can youth be better engaged in school?** Gamification, creativity, and entrepreneurial skills embodied in esports could be the answer. **How do we build deep understanding of gender and cultural inclusion?** Through an immersive esports competition that provides no barriers to participation that other forms of extra-curricular activities may entail. **How can governments and businesses reach young populations to spark behavioural change?** Through product placements in esports events and games, or through esports influencers.

With the velocity of growth of the sector, it is critical that the governance and regulatory structures evolve to mitigate risk, protect vulnerable young participants, and forge trust in esports. As the sector consolidates over the next five years, new agile governance structures will emerge that achieve this need to protect the integrity of the sector and safeguarding of its audiences, while maintaining the entrepreneurial and dynamic essence of the ecosystem. Future digital trends, specifically the metaverse refers to a vision of what online environments, virtual experiences and the internet will become. The realities of what the metaverse will comprise of is not yet clear, but it will be underpinned by social connection and commercialisation. Esports titles have created their own virtual environments already, such as Fortnite, World of Warcraft, yet it is unclear if these established online esports spaces will conflict or intersect with the metaverse. This book provides a timely, practical, and succinct guide for all stakeholders of esports, from participants and fans, to sponsors, media, parents, and regulators. It showcases some relevant case studies that illustrate the current and future direction and role of esports and synthesises the current state of the sector. Esports literacy is important for us all as this burgeoning sector continues to grow and resonate globally.

Notes

1 @Wroetoshaw has 4.3 million Instagram followers and 4 million Twitter followers, alongside 1,079,000 channel views for W2S on Twitch and 16.2 million subscribers on YouTube (as of November 2021).
2 @Gamingwithjen has 948,000 Instagram followers and 308,000 Twitter followers, and 5.23 million subscribers on YouTube (as of November 2021).

References

Ashton, G. (2019, January 16). BitKraft eSports ventures files for $125M venture fund. *The Esports Observer*. https://archive.esportsobserver.com/bitkraft-esports-venture-fund/

Euronews (2021, July 23). Let the games begin! Tokyo 2020 kicks off with manga-inspired opening ceremony. *Euronews*. www.euronews.com/2021/07/23/let-the-games-begin-tokyo-2020-kicks-off-with-manga-inspired-opening-ceremony

Gilchrist, K. (2021, September 14). Emma Raducanu to receive $2.5 million for U.S. Open win – eight times her previous career earnings. *CNBC*. www.cnbc.com/2021/09/14/emma-raducanu-to-earn-2point5-million-for-us-open-win.html

Goh, B. (2021, August 31). Three hours per week: Playtime's over for China's young video gamers. *Reuters*. www.reuters.com/world/china/china-rolls-out-new-rules-minors-online-gaming-xinhua-2021-08-30/

Gough, C. (2021, July 14). Mobile eSports – statistics & facts. *Statista*. www. statista.com/topics/8199/mobile-esports/

IOC. (2018, December 8). Communique of the 7th Olympic summit. *International Olympic Committee*. www.olympic.org/news/communique-of-the-7th-olympic -summit

Ké, X., & Wagner, C. (2020). Global pandemic compels sport to move to esports: Understanding from brand extension perspective. *Managing Sport and Leisure*, 1–6. https://doi.org/10.1080/23750472.2020.1792801

Kelly, S. J., Derrington, S., & Star, S. (2021). Governance challenges in esports: A best practice framework for addressing integrity and wellbeing issues. *International Journal of Sport Policy & Politics*, 1–18. https://doi.org/10.1080/1940694 0.2021.1976812

Ludwig, S., Papenbrock, J., Lachmann, K., & Mesonero, S. (2021, October 20). Let's play! 2021. The European esports market. *Deloitte Insights*. https://www2. deloitte.com/us/en/insights/industry/telecommunications/esports-in-europe.html

Michelli, M. (2018, October 22). Hershey's recruits Ninja and Dr Lupo for release of Reese's pieces candy bar at TwitchCon. *The Esports Observer*. https://archive. esportsobserver.com/hersheys-ninja-dr-lupo-candy-bar/

Newzoo. (2021, July 1). Global games report. *Newzoo*. https://newzoo.com/insights/ trend-reports/newzoo-global-games-market-report-2021-free-version/

Nielsen. (2019). Esports playbook for brands. *Nielsen Sports*. https://nielsensports. com/esports-playbook-for-brands/

Nordland, J. (2021, February 17). Esports 5 years on: Where is the industry headed in the future? *Esports News UK*. https://esports-news.co.uk/2021/02/17/ esports-5-years-on-where-is-the-industry-headed/

Peters, J. (2021, June 2). The Olympics' vision of gaming looks very different from the biggest esports. *The Verge*. www.google.com/amp/s/www.theverge.com/platform/ amp/2021/6/2/22464255/olympic-virtual-series-esports-most-popular-games

Pirker, J. (2020). Video games, technology, and sport: The future is interactive, immersive, and adaptive. In S. L. Schmidt (Ed.), *21st century sports: How technologies will change sports in the digital age* (pp. 263–273). Springer International Publishing.

Sacco, D. (2021, January 9). Riot games announces wild rift esports plans for 2021. *Esports News UK*. https://esports-news.co.uk/2021/01/09/wild-rift-esports-plans- 2021-riot-games/

Takahashi, D. (2020, September 16). Bayes raises $6 million for global esports data platform. *enture Beat*. https://venturebeat.com/2020/09/16/bayes-raises- 6-million-for-global-esports-data-platform/

Index

Note: Page numbers in *italics* indicate figures and page numbers in **bold** indicate tables.

Printed and bound by CPI Group (UK) Ltd, Croydon, CR0 4YY

28/10/2024

01780374-0003